TUDOR WALES

NATHEN AMIN

For Yasmin Shalina

First published 2014

Amberley Publishing
The Hill, Stroud
Gloucestershire, GL5 4EP

www.amberley-books.com

British Library Cataloguing in Publication Data.
A catalogue record for this book is available from the British Library.

ISBN 978 1 4456 1773 2 (paperback)
ISBN 978 1 4456 1791 6 (e-book

Typeset in 10pt on 13pt Sabon.
Typesetting and Origination by Amberley Publishing.
Printed in the UK.

Contents

Coat of Arms of Henry VII in St David's Cathedral.

Introduction

The Tudors are one of history's most infamous families, and the era over which they reigned still captures the public's interest without rival. 'Tudor England' in itself has become a celebrated term that covers many aspects of the era, particularly architecture, the arts and lifestyle. From Henry VII's triumphant rise in 1485 to the demise of his glorious granddaughter Elizabeth in 1603, the 118 years of Tudor rule steered England from the dreary medieval period into a new era of celebrated discovery and advancement. With a fascinating cast of characters shaping extraordinary events which still resonate in parts of the nation today, the Tudors and the world around them have few if any competitors when it comes to sheer drama.

The family that lends its name to the period comprised a usurper, an obese tyrant with six wives, a sickly teenage king, and two warring sisters with the immortal epithets Bloody and Virgin, respectively. When you stage this starring ensemble with the plot features – love triangles, barbaric executions, vicious wars, rowdy revelries and tumultuous religious upheaval – that took place, you are left with a scandalous and dramatic period in history that continues to enthral and excite in equal measure. The tenure in power of the Tudors transformed a warring and fractured medieval kingdom into a genuine global superpower, and their reign encompasses the so-called Elizabethan Golden Age, during which time the Kingdom of England certainly led the world in literature, theatre and exploration. From Raleigh to Shakespeare, Boleyn to Dudley, and the English Bible to the Spanish Armada, the Tudors have succeeded in keeping us entertained for over five centuries.

England became a mighty nation during the reign of sequential Tudors, rapidly developing a self-assurance and assertiveness that would later blossom into the dominant British Empire under their successors. What is often overlooked is that these same Tudors, while coming to encompass all that is still considered great about England and her people, were a Welsh dynasty, with their roots firmly entrenched in the hills beyond Offa's Dyke. As you will discover in this guide, although the royal Tudors were a mixture of Welsh, French and English blood, their male-line ancestors were North Welsh, and they also claimed direct descent from the great South Welsh kings of pre-Conquest Wales.

Much like her larger neighbour, Wales experienced great change under Tudor rule, and many buildings stand today as a legacy to this incredible period of history, when a Welsh family was the most powerful force in the land. This guide will take you on a journey through the beautiful country of Wales and expose you to the hidden gems of the Tudor era, from Harlech Castle in the north to Pembroke Castle in the west, and from the holy Bishop's Palace at Lamphey to the sacred cathedral at St David's. From Dale, Carew and Penmynydd to Raglan, Conwy and Denbigh, every part of Wales has Tudor links, both to the royal Tudors and to their more obscure Welsh ancestors, and this guide will hopefully put you on the path to a true Tudor experience in the Land of their Fathers.

Map of Wales.

Map Key

West Wales

1. The Bosworth Stone
2. Carew Castle
3. Carmarthen Castle
4. St Mary's church, Carmarthen
5. Lamphey Bishop's Palace
6. Laugharne Castle
7. St Wenog's church
8. Mill Bay
9. Pembroke Castle
10. St David's cathedral
11. Tenby
12. St Mary's church, Tenby
13. Tenby Tudor Merchant's House

South Wales

14. Cardiff Castle
15. Hay-on-Wye
16. Llandaff cathedral
17. Neath Abbey
18. Newport cathedral
19. Old Beaupre Castle
20. Oxwich Castle
21. Raglan Castle
22. St Fagans
23. Weobley Castle

North Wales

24. Beaumaris Castle
25. Ty Gwyn, Barmouth
26. Chirk Castle
27. Conwy Castle
28. Plas Mawr, Conwy
29. Denbigh Castle
30. St Marcella's church, Denbigh
31. All Saints church, Gresford
32. Gwydir Castle
33. Harlech Castle
34. St Winefride's Well
35. St Mary's church, Mold
36. Penmynydd
37. St Mary's church, Ruabon
38. Ty Mawr Wybrnant
39. St Giles church, Wrexham
40. Ysbyty Ifan

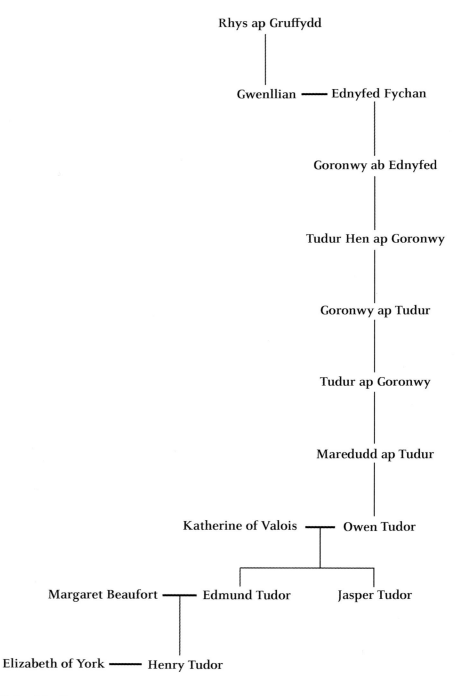

The Welsh Tudors' family tree.

Timeline of Key Events

c. 1170	birth of Ednyfed Fychan, Seneschal to the Prince of Gwynedd in North Wales, who marries Princess Gwenllian, daughter of the Welsh Prince Rhys ap Gruffydd.
c. 1205	birth of Goronwy ap Ednyfed, son of Ednyfed and Gwenllian.
1282	Edward I conquers Wales.
1400	Owain Glyndŵr rebellion in Wales, joined by his Tudur cousins, direct descendants of Goronwy ap Ednyfed.
c. 1400	birth of Owain ap Maredudd ap Tudur, later Owen Tudor.
c. 1428	Owen Tudor secretly marries Queen Katherine of Valois, widow of King Henry V of England.
c. 1430–1432	Edmund Tudor and Jasper Tudor born to Owen Tudor and Queen Katherine.
1456	Edmund Tudor dies at Carmarthen Castle.
1457	birth of Henry Tudor to Edmund's widow Margaret Beaufort at Pembroke Castle.
1485	Henry Tudor defeats King Richard III at Bosworth Field and becomes King of England.
1509	King Henry VII dies and is succeeded by King Henry VIII.
1527	King Henry's 'Great Matter' (his divorce crisis) begins.
1536	Wales is annexed into England by the Act of Union.
1536	Dissolution of the Monasteries.
1547	Edward VI becomes king.
1554	Mary I becomes queen.
1558	Elizabeth I becomes queen.
1588	Defeat of the Spanish Armada.
1603	Elizabeth I dies and House of Tudor is replaced by House of Stuart.

The Bosworth Stone, Abermarlais

In the aftermath of the Battle of Bosworth many areas developed their own myths based on the remarkable victory of Henry Tudor's forces, and Wales was not excluded from these spurious traditions. Situated halfway between Llandeilo and Llandovery on the busy A483 trunk road is a large boulder, which stands just before the entrance to Abermarlais Caravan Park. It is a hefty stone, which distracts you as you hurtle past on your journey from south to north. This rock stands a magnificent 9 feet in height, not including the 3 feet known to be in the ground, securing it.

Known by various names, including Y Garreg Fawr, Maen Cilau and the rather simpler geographical designation of Abermarlais Stone, this unassuming monument stands by the entrance to the former Abermarlais mansion, which was demolished in 1982 after a fire ravaged the property. It is thought that the stone at one time occupied a place within the grounds of the estate but was removed to its current spot in the early Victorian period for reasons now unfathomable. The estate was once under the ownership of Sir Rhys ap Thomas, the great Tudor magnate who ruled over South Wales with the delegated authority of a king. He was a loyal stalwart of Henry Tudor from joining his compatriot's campaign during the march to Bosworth in August 1485. The stone that currently stands close to his former residence is traditionally stated to be a relic of this battle, brought back on Sir Rhys's command as a commemorative trophy of the clash. For this reason the stone has taken on another tag, and has been rechristened the Bosworth Stone.

The Abermarlais estate came in to the ownership of Sir Rhys through his heiress mother, Elizabeth of Abermarlais, a direct descendant of the thirteenth-century North Welsh noble Ednyfed Fychan and his wife, Princess Gwenllian. Not only did this give Sir Rhys a direct lineage to the prestigious Welsh princes, it also ensured he shared a kinship with Henry Tudor, another direct descendant of Ednyfed and Gwenllian.

The Abermarlais lands were eventually requisitioned by the Crown of Henry VIII in 1531, when he executed Sir Rhys's grandson and heir Rhys ap Gruffydd on trumped-up charges of treason, but this stone still stands as a testament to the family's former connections with Abermarlais and the wider Llandeilo area. The likelihood of the stone originating from the Bosworth battlefield is questionable, although the persisting folklore surrounding the object ensures it is a worthwhile diversion from the nearby Dinefwr Castle, the chief seat of Sir Rhys ap Thomas and his regal ancestors.

The Bosworth Stone.

Sir Rhys ap Thomas's coat of arms, Llanwenog church.

Carew Castle

As arguably the largest Tudor house in Wales, Carew Castle was designed to inspire and awe every visitor who stood before its majestic Elizabethan façade, and it still achieves this aim more than 400 years after the property's dismal decline into ruin. Situated in an unusual position on flat, low-lying land next to a scenic tidal pond, the castle can be described as Wales's equivalent to Hampton Court, the much-loved palace of King Henry VIII.

Entrance to the castle is from the car park and along a path which meanders through a grass-covered enclosure, possibly the location of the jousting courtyard, which played a key role in an early sixteenth-century celebration at Carew. The Renaissance house was built on the site of an ancient Norman castle which had been erected around the start of the twelfth century by Gerald de Windsor, a mighty Marcher Lord and husband of the Welsh princess Nest ferch Rhys. This medieval construction subsequently passed into the hands of the prominent de Carew family, and they lend their name to the fortress we see today.

The castle had an uneventful history in the hands of the Carews until it was transferred to the newly flourishing Welsh magnate Rhys ap Thomas in 1480, forever linking the property with this beloved courtier of the first two Tudor monarchs. Affluent with cash and titles after his exploits at the Battle of Bosworth in 1485, Sir Rhys embarked on a

Carew Castle's Elizabethan range.

building program across his territory to demonstrate his new position as the effective viceroy of South Wales, and Carew Castle in particular received lavish attention.

Sir Rhys's intention was to convert this regional medieval castle into an extravagant home suitable for a leading member of the royal court, and this objective he certainly met. His rebuilding programme was dramatically crowned with an extraordinary series of celebrations in 1507, as he rejoiced in his induction into the esteemed Order of the Garter while simultaneously paying tribute to the accession of the Welsh-descended Tudors to the throne of England. The merriments included a grand tournament of jousting, and were considered a great exhibition of the chivalric ideal that Sir Rhys strived to represent.

The event allegedly attracted around 600 knights and lasted for five days; it was a prosperous display, of such splendour that it would continue to be discussed among locals long after the castle lost its glorious grandeur. A modern depiction of this event can be viewed in the lesser hall of the castle in the form of a large hanging tapestry.

It was Sir Rhys who was initially responsible for transforming the fortress into a comfortable mansion, and to achieve this he built the Great Hall on the west side of the castle, including the large oriel window and the multiple fireplaces. The hall is now in a ruinous state, but it is possible to determine the height of the structure and acknowledge the sheer size of the room, which occupies the full length of this side of the castle, bookended by the two Norman towers.

Sir Rhys was also accountable for the addition of a now ruinous three-storey porch over the steps, which would have led into the Great Hall. It is above this porch that the most obvious link between Carew and the Tudors can be found. Engraved into the wall and still decipherable are the royal coat of arms of King Henry VII and the respective arms of his son Prince Arthur and two-time daughter-in-law Katherine of Aragon. The young Prince of Wales had been married to the Spanish Infanta in 1499 and so, as he prematurely died in 1502, the adornment over the porch can be reasonably dated to some point between these dates. There are also the remains of a royal coat of arms on the first-floor fireplace in the lesser hall.

Sir Rhys's grandson Rhys ap Gruffydd was executed for treason in 1531 by an increasingly tyrannical Henry VIII, which brutally severed the link between the families, and the castle passed into the hands of the Crown. It was granted to Elizabethan courtier Sir John Perrot in 1558, and he embarked on the property's second renovation phase, which completed its striking Renaissance outlook. Perrot added the glorious northern range to the castle and it is this extension that provides the archetypical portrayal of Carew Castle today. The range consisted of five separate rooms on the lower floor, while the second floor possessed a long gallery over 40 metres in length – a luxurious addition. The ideal spot for seeing Perrot's extension is from across the pond, where one can view his range in its full magnificence.

The vast mullioned windows, characteristic of the Elizabethan period, can still be observed from within and without the wing, and exhibit the opulence of Perrot's construction. It should be noted that, while Sir Rhys's western additions remain within the original castle walls, Perrot's have no such exterior defence, and demonstrate the emergence of Carew from medieval castle to Elizabethan house. Perrot's treasonous downfall and death in 1592 led the castle into a slow decline, before it was finally abandoned during the Stuart period.

Carew's early Tudor fireplace and window.   Elizabethan mullioned windows.

Sir Rhys ap Thomas's Great Hall exterior.

Carmarthen Castle

Carmarthen Castle is arguably the biggest disappointment among the plethora of medieval ruins in Wales, the remains consisting of one mediocre gatehouse and little else; the one-time regional stronghold has been swallowed up by the modern town that has developed around this former fortress. Considering the past importance of Carmarthen as Wales's oldest town and provincial gateway to the west of the country, it is a shame that little remains today as a visual acknowledgment to its colourful past.

Nonetheless, a Tudor-related visit to the castle remains a necessity, for it was the site of Edmund Tudor's death; the often overlooked father of the first Tudor monarch perished here in November 1456. In his capacity as Earl of Richmond and the beleaguered king's half-brother, Edmund had been posted to Carmarthen on behalf of the House of Lancaster to secure the region's loyalty in the wake of rising Yorkist hostility. Edmund utilised his Welsh roots to gain the submission of the area but, once in possession of Carmarthen Castle, he was soon besieged by a rival Yorkist force, led by William Herbert of Raglan. A force of around 2,000 men was raised throughout Hereford and south-east Wales by Herbert and his cohorts, and on 10 August 1456 they advanced on the castle with orders to suppress and eradicate Edmund's authority. They captured the castle, and Edmund was imprisoned within the dungeon of Carmarthen Castle, demoted from constable to captive.

After suffering imprisonment for around three months, Edmund passed away on 1 November 1456 from what appears to have been an outbreak of the plague, although it may have been from wounds received in the earlier clash with Herbert's force. His wife, Margaret Beaufort, was pregnant at the time, and Edmund would never get to see his son Henry, the future King of England. As an earl of the realm and a respected Welsh noble, Edmund was still granted a reasonable burial in spite of the uncertainty surrounding the governance of the kingdom, and was interred at the Greyfriars church just outside the Carmarthen town walls. His tomb would later be removed to St David's Cathedral under the reign of his grandson King Henry VIII.

Today the castle can be accessed from Nott Square; from here you approach the 13-metre-high gatehouse, but once beyond this bleak entranceway there is nothing of note except a few walls and an unexceptional south-east tower, admittedly with scenic views across the River Tywi. Even so, Carmarthen Castle remains a key part of the Tudor story due to Edmund's tragic downfall, and is worthy of a visit when passing through on the way to West Wales.

St Peter's Church, Carmarthen

Carmarthen is one of the oldest towns in Britain, a continuation of the Roman Moridunum, and St Peter's church remains the earliest extant building in the region that is still used for its original purpose. The exact date of foundation is unknown, but it appears to have existed from at least the early twelfth century, with today's structure still containing elements from the thirteenth century. The prominent tower is a fifteenth-century addition, while the south aisle was constructed during the Tudor period. It is this aisle which holds an acute connection to the Tudor dynasty as the resting place of Sir Rhys ap Thomas; his alabaster tomb was placed here in 1538 after the Dissolution of the Monasteries disrupted his original resting place at the nearby Greyfriars monastery.

Greatly rewarded by his distant kinsman King Henry VII in gratitude for his unyielding allegiance during the reign of the first Tudor monarch, Sir Rhys governed South Wales with a kingly assurance, which he maintained until his death in 1525. He was interred in Greyfriars, close to the king's own father Edmund Tudor, but both tombs were removed during the Dissolution. Sir Rhys's tomb occupies a position which is significantly less exposed than Edmund's; it is placed in a quiet corner with two sides lamentably positioned next to a wall, which denies the visitor the opportunity to circumvent the mighty monument. The effigy is heavily weathered despite its attempted restoration by a later descendant, although the three ravens that were prominent in his coat of arms are still identifiable. The tomb bears the inscription: 'Here lies the remains of Sir Rhys ap Thomas K. G. who fought at Bosworth Field'. Interest in Sir Rhys has certainly increased recently because of his possible role in the death of King Richard III at Bosworth Field in 1485, and there are hopes that this could result in his tomb receiving a higher degree of decorum than it has been accorded over the last century.

St Peter's also maintains two other Tudor-era connections, which enhances the church's status as a credible sixteenth-century location. Walter Devereux, Earl of Essex, is believed to have been buried in an unmarked grave under the chancel in 1576. Devereux had been a loyal courtier of Queen Elizabeth I, and controversially and often violently served her interests in Ireland where he had been appointed Earl Marshal. His son was Robert Devereux, who later gained notoriety as a keen favourite of the queen before his execution for treason in 1601. In 1555, the church also played a role in the trial of Robert Ferrar, Bishop of St David's, a devout Protestant who was condemned as a heretic at St Peter's and sentenced to death by burning. This gruesome act was carried out in Carmarthen marketplace, where a plaque today commemorates the event, a consequence of the persecution of Protestants under the reign of Queen Mary Tudor. A nineteenth-century marble plaque can also be viewed in the consistory court; it states that the bishop was burnt for 'adhering to the protestant religion', a reminder that the turmoil of England's religious strife was equally felt in the heart of Wales.

Above left: Tomb of Sir Rhys ap Thomas, St Peter's church.

Above right: St Peter's church tower, Carmarthen.

Effigy of Sir Rhys ap Thomas.

Lamphey Bishop's Palace

The quiet village of Lamphey is the home of a magnificent ruin: the crumbling Bishop's Palace, a plush retreat which belonged to the incumbent Bishop of St David's. During the commencement of the Wars of the Roses in the 1450s, Edmund Tudor was repositioned in to West Wales in order to ensure the king's authority in the area was upheld during a time when local Welsh landowners appeared to be on the cusp of armed rebellion. As half-brother to the king through their mutual mother Katherine of Valois, and as a descendant of the great Welsh princes through his father Owen, Edmund was the ideal candidate for such an assignment, and based himself at the palatial home of the bishop. It is believed to have been at Lamphey Palace that Edmund honeymooned with his young bride Margaret Beaufort, and it is a further possibility that it was at his Pembrokeshire headquarters that his son, the future King Henry VII, was conceived sometime during 1456.

Although the palace is now a ruin, the substantial remains allow the visitor to visualise the property during its opulent fifteenth-century peak, the plain outer wall concealing the affluent splendour inside. The location was, and still is, situated in the middle of sprawling forest, which, together with the bountiful fish ponds and vast orchards, ensured anything the earl required was openly available for his convenience. The living quarters of Edmund and Margaret can be found in the furthest corner of the site, where the bulk of the architectural ruins still stubbornly stand. The western hall can be reached by external steps from the ground floor, while a spectacularly intact cellar dwells in the darkness underneath the de Gower hall. The pleasant vista from both halls is of the Pembrokeshire countryside, a quiet area of solace suitable for the pious Lady Margaret to reflect in.

The palace also played host to Sir Rhys ap Thomas in 1507, in anticipation of the magnate's great celebrations at his nearby residence of Carew Castle. The incumbent bishop, Robert Sherborne, personally blessed Sir Rhys and the large retinue of knights who were due to take part in the festivities. The chapel was rebuilt during the tenure of Edward Vaughan between 1509 and 1522, the bishop embarking on a similar renovation programme as the one he had initiated at St David's Cathedral. Notable from this period is the large eastern wall of the chapel, and evidence of a large perpendicular window is unmistakable. By 1536 an inventory of the Bishop's Palace described twenty-seven rooms, with the bishop's own chamber in particular singled out due to its lavish furnishings. In August 1546 the palace was requisitioned by the Crown of Henry VIII before coming under the control of the Devereux family for the remainder of the Tudor period; this family were responsible for the rounded Elizabethan chimney in the old hall.

Lamphey is an undeniably romantic location and offers an abundance of serenity to the visitor. It is easy to see why this wonderfully atmospheric palace was considered the ideal accommodation for a king's brother, a palatial retreat that played its part in the rise of the Tudors.

Laugharne Castle

Built overlooking the River Taf estuary in Carmarthenshire, Laugharne Castle is the ruinous remains of a former Tudor mansion built within the confines of a Norman Marcher fortress. Often attacked by the native Welsh princes during the turbulent Middle Ages, the castle was somewhat rescued from its increasingly derelict state in 1584 when Queen Elizabeth I granted the fortress to Sir John Perrot, a courtier rumoured to be an illegitimate son of Henry VIII and thus possibly the queen's half-brother. Perrot had been born around 1528, and allegedly resembled the great king in both appearance and temperament, enjoying a degree of advancement in the varying courts of the monarch's children. In the reign of Elizabeth he was particularly prominent, regularly being appointed to positions in Ireland during the Elizabethan conquest of the troublesome island.

Perrot began to renovate the castle, and transformed the dreary and battle-hardened site into an opulent mansion, although it was later said to have suffered from poor workmanship. There are still a few signs of Perrot's castle, notably the northern range, which stands between the two large circular towers that bookend these apartments. In the centre of the range is the protruding stair tower; its square-headed windows in particular betray its Tudor roots. The inner gatehouse, which allows access in to the courtyard, is particularly striking, and this was raised to its impressive height under Perrot – high entrance archways are typical of the late Tudor period. The ruins which would have comprised the Great Hall and southern-range chambers can also be viewed looking outward towards the estuary; they are distinguishable by the gap, which once housed a large oriel window to provide light, and the fireplace, which provided the heat. Around the site runs a rushing stream, with an ancient stone bridge which has provided a charming pedestrian crossing point for many centuries. Today it is a welcome resting spot from which to view the exterior of the great castle without any visual interruption from dreary modern architecture, a rarity in this day and age.

This Elizabethan mansion would not prosper due to Perrot's alarming downfall: in 1592 he found himself arrested for treason and sentenced to death. He had accumulated great wealth but also a number of enemies at court, and would die imprisoned before his judicial sentence could be carried out. Laugharne Castle stands today as a legacy to Perrot's brief intention of building a magnificent Tudor palace on the edge of Carmarthen Bay – ironically, today it is as ruined as Perrot's own reputation was at the end of his life.

St Wenog's Church, Llanwenog

The parish church of Llanwenog is situated in a small, rustic village roughly ten minutes outside the university town of Lampeter. Its looming tower is prominent from a few miles away among the multitude of picturesque green hills typical of this part of Mid Wales. This battlemented tower has all the hallmarks of a medieval construction, and is certainly unusual in its placement – its appearance is more typical of a strategic fortress than of the cornerstone of a rural parish church. The tower includes a vantage point for a watchman, a curious defensive addition, ostensibly in anticipation of any possible military activity in the area – unlikely as that may seem in this isolated part of Wales. The tower was built shortly after the Battle of Bosworth in 1485 under the orders of Sir Rhys ap Thomas, Henry Tudor's loyal and all-powerful right-hand man in Wales. Sir Rhys had provided a large retinue of men at Bosworth, and there's a high probability that the village of Llanwenog in the heart of his lands supplied a respectable number of soldiers to the cause of Henry Tudor, perhaps prompting the construction as a gesture of gratitude to the villagers. While Tudor roses adorn the lychgate and the Lady chapel roof, the clearest indicator of the tower's origins lie above the west doorway. Below the window can be seen the portcullis badge of King Henry VII's Beaufort ancestors, while displayed above the doorway is Sir Rhys's own coat of arms, represented within the Order of the Garter emblem he was entitled to display after his inclusion as a knight in 1505.

St Wenog's church tower.

Mill Bay

After Henry Tudor, exiled Earl of Richmond, was lauded as the heir to the Lancastrian claim, it was only a matter of time before he attempted to land back in England from his place of refuge in Brittany and France. His first attempt to land in the south-west of England in 1483 had ended in a farcical failure, and cost his ally and rival claimant Henry, Duke of Buckingham, his head. Henry launched another invasion two years later, and on this occasion aimed to land in his native West Wales, as good an area as any to draw much-needed support to his banner. That Henry was descended from a respected Welsh bloodline is undisputed, and, when his Pembrokeshire birth and his uncle Jasper's standing in the region as a deposed Earl of Pembroke are taken into consideration, the decision to seek out a landing point in this extremity of the island was certainly shrewd.

Henry's disparate and primarily mercenary force landed in Mill Bay on 7 August 1485 just before sunset, close to the village of Dale. This marked the beginning of Henry's arduous march through Wales and England to meet the forces of King Richard III, ultimately at the Battle of Bosworth Field on 22 August. The Pembrokeshire antiquarian George Owen recorded in 1602 that it was 'neare this point of Dale, between yt and the town of Dale, landed King Henry 7th and his Armye from Brytanne when he came into England and conquered King Richard the third'. According to the late fifteenth-century chronicler Robert Fabyan, when Henry landed back on Welsh soil for the first time in

Mill Bay.

fourteen years he kneeled upon the ground and recited Psalm 43 in Latin, emotionally pleading, 'Judge me, O God, and distinguish my cause.' Upon completion of the biblical verse, the devout Henry piously made the sign of the cross and commanded his followers 'boldly in the name of God and Saint George to set forward'. It was a rousing call to arms, and his primarily French and Scottish force trailed their leader inland and onwards toward battle, acquiring further reinforcements from the Welsh along the way.

Present-day Dale is still a minor village of only 200 people, and is within short walking distance of the coast. Access to Mill Bay can be found by following the Pembrokeshire Coastal Path from the prominent St Ann's Head lighthouse. The cove itself is rather secluded, and the surrounding sandstone promontories would have helped to shelter the landing force, a natural haven for an invading force to alight without attracting attention. Crucially the bay was out of sight of Dale Castle, which allowed the force ample opportunity to clamber up the steep hill from the water without detection. A plaque commemorates Henry's landing with the statement, in English and then Welsh, 'Henry Tudor, Earl of Richmond, landed at Mill bay on 7 August 1485 with his 55 ships and 4,000 men landing at Dale.'

Plaque in Dale, near Mill Bay.

Pembroke Castle

Of the plethora of Tudor locations in Wales, one could argue that none enjoy the strength of connection to the great royal dynasty which Pembroke Castle proudly boasts. It was in this mighty regional fortress that Henry Tudor, Earl of Richmond from birth and future King of England, was born one winter night in the mid-fifteenth century, as the country around him descended into the brutal civil war known to posterity as the Wars of the Roses. No one at the time could have foreseen that this small newborn would benefit from the escalating tensions between the houses of York and Lancaster to become the first monarch of England's greatest family, in what has to be one of the most unlikely outcomes in British history.

A castle has been at Pembroke since before the Norman Conquest, although, in a situation replicated throughout the area from the eleventh century, it was the Marcher lords empowered by William the Conqueror who truly began to fortify the location. Standing on a rocky promontory beside the Cleddau Estuary, with convenient maritime access to the Celtic Sea and Ireland, Pembroke Castle enjoyed a status as an invaluable stronghold, from which successive generations of magnates conducted their political and military activities. Perhaps the greatest noble to possess Pembroke was Sir William Marshal, 1st Earl of Pembroke, who became one of the most powerful men in England and beyond during the early thirteenth century. It is perhaps Marshal above all who is most responsible for Pembroke's transformation into a domineering and impenetrable fortress. One of the peculiar claims that those who held Pembroke would regularly make was the curious fact that it had never been captured by the native Welsh in battle, and had even remained secure during the Glyndŵr uprising in 1400, a testament to the security and safety the castle offered to its lord.

Tudor involvement in Pembroke Castle began when the fortress was presented to Jasper Tudor in 1452 as a core part of his new Earldom of Pembroke, a title which had been bestowed upon him by his compassionate, if politically and mentally unstable, half-brother King Henry VI. After his brother Edmund's death at Carmarthen Castle in November 1456, Jasper endeavoured to offer protection to his pregnant widow Margaret Beaufort, a vulnerable young teenager of only thirteen years old. Placing her in his care at Pembroke, it was in one of the outer wards to the west of the gatehouse, on 28 January 1457, that Margaret gave birth to her son, a child without a father but in the devoted care of his mother and uncle.

In addition to her young age, Margaret was noted to have a small frame not suited to the rigours of childbirth; by all accounts it was a difficult pregnancy and probably rendered her infertile for the remainder of her life, as there were no other instances of her bearing children, in spite of two further marriages. The birth is traditionally stated to have taken place in one of the outer guard chambers which flank the great gatehouse. Consisting of three storeys, a fireplace and a garderobe it is an unusually subdued location for the birth of a noble child, and there has not been a sufficient explanation as to why the birth allegedly took place here. Today this momentous occasion is commemorated by a waxwork exhibition of the nativity scene, depicting Margaret Beaufort, the newborn Henry and two ladies-in-waiting shortly after the birth; the guard chamber itself has been proudly named the Henry VII Tower.

The child was sickly soon after his birth, and good care by both his mother and the attendant nurses seems to be the core reason for the newborn not becoming yet another statistic for the alarmingly high infant mortality rates of the period. Although the baby was christened Henry, a regal English name and probably in tribute to the child's half-uncle Henry VI, a later tradition suggested the original name was in fact Owain. Although no contemporary evidence exists to corroborate this account, it is interesting to note nevertheless that Welsh poetic prophecies suggested an Owain would come to lead the Welsh to freedom from the English as their *Mab Darogan*, or son of prophecy. While it is a possibility the legend could contain a shred of truth, particularly as the child's still-living paternal grandfather was named Owain, the likelihood is that it was an apocryphal tale from later generations of the Welsh gentry, attempting to further increase the acceptance of the later Tudors in Wales through the circulation of such an emotive myth. By blood Henry of Richmond was one quarter French, one quarter Welsh and half English, but with his birthplace and paternal grandfather's pedigree it was always expected that the Welsh people would proudly claim Harri Tudur as their own, an acceptance which would remain consistent until the advent of modern Welsh twentieth-century nationalism.

The birth of Henry Tudor, Pembroke Castle.

Henry would spend his first few years living comfortably at the castle, until national politics had an adverse effect on his peaceful existence. The increasingly hostile battle for supremacy between the House of Lancaster, to which he and his uncle Jasper belonged, and the aspiring Yorkist faction had descended into open warfare during 1459, and two years later the conflict was brought to Pembroke. In February 1461 Henry's grandfather Owen Tudor had been killed at the Battle of Mortimer's Cross in Herefordshire and by September Jasper's castle at Pembroke was besieged by Yorkist forces led by Sir William Herbert. With Jasper forced to flee in order to escape execution at the hands of his enemies, the constable of the castle peacefully surrendered the fortress to the Yorkists, and the four-year-old Earl of Richmond fell into the hands of Herbert. Henry would remain in the guardianship of Herbert for the next decade, finding himself relocated from Pembroke to Raglan Castle until Sir William's violent death in 1469. Pembroke would briefly feature once more in Henry Tudor's early life when its fortifications provided respite for him and Jasper in 1471 on their way to Tenby during their incredible flight into exile.

Once he became King Henry VII, Pembroke Castle did not feature highly among his immediate concerns, although his son would temporarily draw attention to the Tudor

The Great Keep, Pembroke Castle.

Henry VII Tower, Pembroke Castle.

connection with this West Walian fortress when Anne Boleyn was invested as the Marquess of Pembroke on 1 September 1532 in anticipation of her eventual progression to queen. The ceremony was presided over by Henry VIII himself at Windsor Castle and was attended by the highest-ranking magnates in the realm, who were eager to seem agreeable to the king's desire to take a new wife. The association of Pembroke with Anne was designed by Henry and was a typical example of Tudor propaganda to integrate Anne into the family, and the ceremony itself was effectively a coronation.

Pembroke Castle covers a vast area that is possibly unrivalled in South Wales. The outer ward is largely empty as previous buildings have long crumbled, although excavations in the early twentieth century unearthed Jasper Tudor's private house, which he had built during his tenure as Earl of Pembroke in the late fifteenth century. In the inner ward stands a heavily weathered oriel window on the west wall of the solar, a private room for the benefit of the lord, which Jasper was also responsible for adding, although its one-time splendour can no longer be appreciated.

Unquestionably, the premier attraction of Pembroke Castle is Sir William Marshal's Great Keep, construction of which was begun in 1204. It is a behemoth of a structure and still stands proudly defiant as one of the largest of its kind still standing anywhere in the UK. The keep is 75 feet tall with a sturdy base 20 feet thick. The tower contains five storeys, with a single spiral staircase which was initially reached by an external timber staircase to the first floor. The view from the domed summit is breathtaking, and commanding views of the surrounding landscape reduce the observer to an awestruck silence. The tower would have been the greatest structure that many generations of the local community would have encountered, and certainly would have been viewed with a degree of wonder by the young Henry Tudor during his brief childhood stay at the castle.

Pembroke can legitimately claim to be the birthplace of the Tudor dynasty, yet sadly lacks the reputation and promotion that other Tudor locations in England enjoy. While it can be expected that this medieval stronghold will never rival a Hampton Court or Hever Castle for tourists, it certainly deserves to be included on the itinerary of any Tudor enthusiast. There has been a concerted effort of late to promote Pembroke, with greater focus on the title 'Birthplace of the Tudor Dynasty', and a recent development has been the announcement of a paved Tudor rose in the town centre.

Opposite: Henry VII Tower exterior, Pembroke Castle.

St David's Cathedral

St David's Cathedral is a location in Wales which requires no detailed introduction; it is a large place of Christian worship founded by the eponymous saint in the sixth century. Standing 115 feet tall and 300 feet in length, this massive structure is awe-inspiring in spite of its position built in to the valley floor.

Named after the patron saint of Wales, St David's Cathedral can be considered the spiritual home of the Welsh nation, and is a grand structure that takes the visitor's breath away upon the first sighting from Tower Gate House. The status of St David's was substantially bolstered in 1123 when a papal bull from Pope Calixtus II decreed that 'two pilgrimages to St David's is equal to one to Rome, and three pilgrimages to one to Jerusalem'.

With its tumultuous history, littered with blood, murder and royalty, it seems fitting that a Tudor is buried next to the high altar in a place of privilege within sight of a prestigious ancestor. The tomb in question is that of Edmund Tudor, Earl of Richmond and father of King Henry VII, and was safely removed here from the Greyfriars in Carmarthen after the Dissolution of the Monasteries under his notorious grandson Henry VIII.

It could be considered that this cuboid tomb, minus an alabaster effigy, is the closest Wales has to an English royal sarcophagus. The circumstances surrounding Edmund's tomb are uncertain, and historical sources are scarce, but it could be safely assumed that, as grandfather of the current king, it was a political necessity to ensure the safekeeping of the earl's remains once his resting place at Carmarthen was destroyed, and his memory had to be honoured by placing him in a position of privilege in Wales. Whether these orders came from Henry VIII, a man who seemingly never paid much attention to his Welsh roots, is debatable, but certainly someone in some degree of authority deemed it a wise decision. The rectangular design of the tomb is minimalistic compared to many similar conceptions, and it incorporates a brass effigy, as opposed to a more opulent alabaster depiction. The royal coat of arms of his son is particularly prominent on the tomb, as well as that of Owen Tudor.

The inscription reads, 'Under this marble stone here inclosed resteth the bones of that most noble lord Edmond Earl of Richmond father and brother to kings, the which departed out of this world in our lord God MCCCCLVI the third of the month of November: on whose soul Almighty Jesu have mercy.' Another notable tomb, albeit one from the twelfth century rather than the sixteenth, is that of the renowned South Welsh king, Rhys ap Gruffydd – or, as he's better known, The Lord Rhys. As Prince of Deheubarth, Rhys reclaimed sovereignty over much of South Wales from the aggressive Norman Marcher Lords who had violently seized large sections of the region. His daughter Gwenllian was married to Ednyfed Fychan, a prominent North Welsh noble who effectively operated as the chief advisor to the princes of Gwynedd. It was through this marriage that the Tudors were directly descended; thus Rhys ap Gruffydd was in fact the great-great-great-great-great-great-grandfather of the man resting in the tomb mere feet away.

The most noted personality connected with the cathedral during the Tudor period was Edward Vaughan, appointed to the Bishopric of St David's on 13 January 1509, a mere two weeks before the death of King Henry VII. Ostensibly a Welshman, or at least of Welsh origin, he was a Cambridge scholar who had served in various roles at St Paul's Cathedral in London before his promotion to West Wales. Taking up his office in July that year, Vaughan worked diligently to create a new chapel and to remodel the existing Lady chapel. His episcopacy was notable for his patronage of the Holy Trinity chapel and in particular the fan-vaulted roof, typical of the Tudor period and similar to that at King's College in Cambridge, with which he may have been personally familiar. On the walls of this chapel he also ensured he paid tribute to the prominent Welshmen of his day, placing the arms of Henry VII and Sir Rhys ap Thomas in a conspicuous and revered place, including the king's arms on the ceiling. He died in 1522 and is buried in the chapel for which he is today remembered, an ostentatious display of pre-Reformation Tudor ecclesiastical architecture. One last feature to observe is the wooden nave roof, known to have been built around the Reformation in 1540.

Tomb of Edmund Tudor, St David's Cathedral.

Tenby

Tenby is a thriving seaside resort on the Pembrokeshire coast, and has managed to retain its traditional charm in spite of the droves of tourists that can be found flocking through its streets each summer. Behind the spades and sandcastles, however, the quaint little town possesses a magnificent Tudor history, which is often overlooked by visitors eager to participate only in the recreational activities the town provides, rather than the historical aspects. Tenby is thought to have become settled around the ninth century, and would eventually come under the administrative control of the Norman earls of Pembroke, from the notable de Clare family in the twelfth century to the pre-eminent Marshal clan of the thirteenth.

By the middle of the fifteenth century and the unlikely rise of the Tudor family, Tenby was a significant provincial port with a sizable population, and earned a living from the bountiful harbour. The Welsh name, Dinbych-y-Pysgod, is commonly accepted to translate as 'little fortress of the fishes', leaving no doubt as to the importance that the sea, and its abundant supply of fish, played in the growth of Tenby. Its proximity to the open ocean was acknowledged by the new Earl of Pembroke in the 1450s, an appreciation of its geographic location that would transform the town from obscure outpost to a strategic fortress during the tumultuous Wars of the Roses.

Tenby harbour.

As half-brother to the beleaguered Lancastrian King Henry VI, Jasper Tudor and his elder brother Edmund had faced a life of uncertain obscurity until their exalted sibling received them into his royal household and took an active interest in their upbringing. The king's mother, Queen Katherine of Valois, had been widowed at the young age of twenty-two and soon found love with a member of her household, the North Walian Owain ap Maredudd ap Tudur, subsequently known as Owen Tudor. Suffice to say a woman in Katherine's position was not expected to cavort with men, much less a lowly Welsh servant with fewer rights than his English counterparts. Nonetheless the couple persisted in their secret existence away from prying eyes, and through this clandestine union became the parents of four children, including Jasper and Edmund. After Katherine's death at the age of thirty-five in 1437, Owen was incarcerated due to his apparent intransigence in illegally marrying the king's mother, and the two children became wards of King Henry and were favourably raised. Once Jasper had reached adulthood he was ennobled as the Earl of Pembroke, a semi-royal title that rewarded him with vast estates in West Wales. As a result, Jasper would remain unwavering in his loyalty to his sovereign over the next two decades, in the face of a vicious challenge for supremacy from the House of York, and Tenby would be a key strategic base from which to plan his campaigns.

Jasper's first implementation once he became the Earl of Pembroke was to expand on the existing thirteenth-century walls that surrounded the town, demanding that the fortifications that his predecessor William de Valence had constructed be substantially strengthened, in order to withstand any potential threat. To signify his desire, Jasper officially signed Letters Patent on 1 December 1457 ordering the commencement of the refortification.

The earl's insistence on solidifying the walls indicates that he was probably aware that tensions in England over the right to govern the realm could escalate into a civil war at any given moment, and his judgement would later be vindicated. Jasper issued orders to the mayor and the town's burgesses to progress with the reinforcement, and offered to fund half of the rebuilding himself, a concession formally noted in the Letters Patent.

Jasper was also adamant that the mayor hire the best carpenters and masons in the area, and pay them competitive rates to ensure the work was done to such a calibre as to be compliant with his needs. One other stipulation set out in his Letters Patent agreement with the town was that any fines issued to persons causing damage to the walls would be reinvested for the purposes of whatever repair or maintenance the walls needed. It was the strategy of a man who wished to ensure the walls were sturdy and professionally made, while also becoming self-reliant with regards to funding.

The primary improvement to the walls was in their depth, with certain sections ordered by Jasper to be thickened by an incredible 6 feet. The height of the ramparts was also increased. In addition, Jasper arranged for a new moat to be dug outside the new walls, said to measure an almost impenetrable 30 feet across and certainly designed to be treacherous to any potential invader. A new tower was built into the walls, and the existing turrets were again raised higher, complementing the additional walkways that were integrated into the defensive structure.

His enhancement of the walls ensured that Tenby would be an extremely difficult place to subdue in the event of a siege, and would not only serve to protect himself but also the common residents of the town. Tenby had become a fortress intended to withstand any attack from aggressive forces, a situation Jasper certainly expected as the country tumbled towards the Wars of the Roses. He proceeded to fortify other castles within his remit, and although none were improved to the extent of Tenby his West Wales project transformed the region into a safe haven for Lancastrian interests.

The wars between the rival royal houses of York and Lancaster finally erupted into prolonged violent conflict in 1459 and, as half-brother to the head of the Lancastrian faction, Jasper was intimately involved as a commander of his Welsh forces. It was to Tenby that a defeated and disheartened Jasper retreated in February 1461 after his defeat at the Battle of Mortimer's Cross in Herefordshire, his army crushed by the forces of the future King Edward IV, head of the House of York. Disastrously for the Tudors, Jasper's father Owen was captured and ruthlessly beheaded at Hereford that same day. Jasper contemplated this heartbreak behind the safety of his Tenby walls and, in one particular correspondence to his kinsmen in North Wales, expressed his desire for revenge, concluding with the line 'written at our town of Tenby'. It was certainly a location in which he felt safe during times of danger.

He would again seek sanctuary from his foes in the town a decade later, when another Lancastrian defeat at the Battle of Tewkesbury in May 1471 resulted in his being pursued through South Wales by the Yorkists. He had recently retaken possession of his fourteen-year-old nephew Henry Tudor, and both boy and uncle fled to Tenby. With the capable assistance of Mayor Thomas White, it is alleged that the fugitive party hid in tunnels underneath the town before being led to a ship which was waiting in the harbour, possibly the mayor's own barque. Tenby's location on the most westerly part of Wales allowed the Tudors to quickly navigate from the harbour into the Bristol Channel and from there out into the tempestuous Celtic Sea towards their destination: France. The turbulent weather disrupted their voyage and drove them off course. They eventually landed at Le Conquet in Brittany, then an independent duchy separate from France. It would prove to be their home for the next twelve years. The Tudors had had a narrow escape, and Jasper had succeeded in saving his teenage nephew's life by the smallest of margins by utilising the security that Tenby's man-made defences and geographic setting provided him.

Once Jasper's nephew became king, the Earl of Pembroke was in a position to be rewarded for his unyielding loyalty to Henry, and in turn he ensured he used his advanced position to reward those who had offered him assistance. Jasper issued his second Letters Patent at some point between 1486 and 1495, reconfirming each of Tenby's previous charters, which had been dispensed of under his predecessors. He signed the document, at his newly acquired stately home of Sudeley, '*Jasper Regum frater et patruus Dux Bedfordie Comes Pembrochie Dominus Glamorgane et Morgane Justiciarius South Wallie ac locum tenens Domini Regis terre sue Hibernie*', reflecting his new titles of Duke of Bedford, Lord of Glamorgan and Morgannwg, Justiciar of South Wales and Lieutenant of Ireland. The town of Tenby had been faithful to Jasper, and he duly rewarded its people while he was at his most powerful.

The town has undergone the evolutionary regeneration that blights every town in the UK today but, as a historic port with many listed buildings, it is still possible to gauge the feel of the town during the days in which Jasper and Henry escaped through its narrow

Plaque on Crackwell Street.

Plaque on Boots, Tenby.

streets. The predominant feature on the approach to the town is the wall, which stands resolute along the South Parade; the turret that stands on the junction with White Lion Street is notable for the Tudor-rose-adorned county flag of Pembrokeshire, which flutters in the wind atop the fortification. Towards the centre of the South Parade wall is the imposing Barbican gate, a focal point of Tenby's tourism trade as the favoured entrance into the old town.

Known colloquially as the self-explanatory Five Arches, the larger arch is the very gateway from the fifteenth century that the Tudors would have passed through on their way in and out of the town. This particular arch was designed as a further security implementation, with the tight angle ensuring that attacking forces would not be able to ram the gate with the run-up needed to cause maximum damage.

Although the original slots can still be viewed, unfortunately the gate no longer possesses its portcullis; once more, however, the design allows one to picture how this defensive gateway must have appeared. Famed antiquarian John Leland mentioned Tenby in one of his highly reputed works in 1540, describing it as 'a walled town hard on the Severn Sea in Pembrokeshire ... the town is strongly walled and well gated, every gate having a portcullis made entirely of iron'. Further down this South Parade wall stands a plaque on the barricade, inscribed with '1588 E. R. 30', a commemoration of the rebuilding of this section in anticipation of the Spanish Armada. This is not the only link to Elizabeth I in the town, for there is a modern sign outside the market that celebrates her granting a charter in 1581, which promoted Tenby into a borough.

Elsewhere the town contains other Tudor connections. Mayor Thomas White was a successful merchant and was known to live in a large town house opposite St Mary's church. Today the four-storey Georgian building contains a Boots pharmacy, but, underneath this present building, the tunnels said to have contained Jasper and Henry in 1471 still exist. The tunnels are said to have run directly under Crackwell Street behind Boots until they reached the water's edge, providing an ideal route of escape for the Tudors. A small and difficult-to-decipher brass panel on the front of Boots states, 'By tradition Henry Tudor with his uncle Jasper Earl of Pembroke was hidden in the cellar on this site before escaping to Brittany in 1471. In 1485 he landed at Dale and defeated Richard III at Bosworth to take the throne as the first Tudor monarch.' The plaque is adorned with the Tudor rose and a Welsh dragon. A commemorative blue plaque on Crackwell Street was erected by the Tenby Civic Society and, in rather simpler but clearer terms, states, 'It is said that Henry Tudor (later King Henry VII) escaped through a tunnel here in 1471 when he fled to France.' Their legacy is also found a few yards down from Boots in the very heart of Tenby – the popular area, now rechristened Tudor Square – while St Catherine's Island was also once the personal property of Jasper Tudor in his role as Earl of Pembroke.

Tenby is arguably the most intriguing and atmospheric location for the modern visitor to frequent, a bountiful town replete with fifteenth- and sixteenth-century links. The town walls were built by Jasper Tudor, the tunnels hid Henry Tudor, and the town charter was confirmed by Elizabeth Tudor. It's certainly an ideal setting for a history-laden hot summer's day exploring the delightful Tudor sites, and is greatly recommended to all Tudor enthusiasts.

St Mary's Church, Tenby

When stood in the heart of Tenby, or indeed outside the coastal resort, the one distinguishing feature within the town that can be determined from all vantage points is the spectacular spire of the central St Mary's church. Rising dominantly over Tudor Square, St Mary's has been a constant in the religious history of the town since at least the thirteenth century.

The church was first recorded by the renowned Norman-Welsh cleric Giraldus Cambrensis in 1210 when he was rector of the parish, after he complained that he was not receiving his rightful share of fish as befitted his role. The church was extensively rebuilt towards the end of the thirteenth century, almost certainly related to the destruction caused to the town by the Welsh Prince Llywelyn ap Gruffydd, when he sacked it in 1260.

By the fifteenth century Tenby had become a prosperous trading port inhabited by a plethora of eager merchants importing and exporting their goods from the harbour, their increasing wealth reflected not only in the extensive rebuilding of their houses but also in the reconstruction of St Mary's. Jasper Tudor's interest in Tenby in the mid-fifteenth century also ensured that the status of the seaport was further enhanced, and he would certainly have been a visitor to the parish church during his extended stays in his fortified town. Due to its prominent role and position in the locality, it is therefore no surprise to discover that St Mary's has a charming Tudor past worth exploring.

The large tower is a local landmark, which breaks through the Tenby skyline without rival, and on certain days can be climbed, offering the visitor breathtaking views across the harbour from the top. Such an experience offers a unique observation on the tight layout of the narrow streets, which still follow their medieval lines. The spire which adorns the tower is a later addition but increases the overall height to an impressive 152 feet, ensuring St Mary's enjoys a status as one of Wales's most magnificent medieval constructions.

Today, one primarily enters the church via the porch that runs alongside the north aisle but if you enter through the west churchyard you will be faced with the naturally named West Door, a worn yet fascinating example of Tudor architecture. This was not originally the external entry point of the western section of the church, as this side of the building also initially possessed a porch of larger proportions to those still seen on the north and south sides of the church. This opulent entranceway was regrettably demolished during the nineteenth century but the actual doorway into the nave is still worth viewing.

The wooden door itself may not be Tudor but it stands within a double-ogee frame that is characteristic of the 1490s Gothic style in which it was built. The ogee is essentially an upward curve that creates an artistic arch, and this west porch of St Mary's is one that would have been resplendent with Tudor imagery shortly after construction. Although the outer doorway is no longer present, it was recorded that the Latin inscription on the external surface read, 'Blessed be God in his gifts.' Although the inner ogee design is now severely weathered it can still be determined that this bears the same engraving. The outer door was also known to have contained the heraldic shields of Henry Tudor

The tomb of the Whites, St Mary's church, Tenby.

Robert Recorde Plaque, St Mary's church.

and his beloved mother Margaret Beaufort in addition to their respective coats of arms. Although these no longer exist, one can still view a plethora of small Tudor roses on the surviving ogee door frame, ornamentation that almost certainly was added around the time of construction in 1496.

Inside the church there are two main attractions with Tudor connections to view, both of which can be found in the fifteenth-century St Thomas's Chapel in the south-east of the building. On the wall to the right of the entrance into the chapel is situated a superb memorial to the eminent Tudor scholar Robert Recorde, a native of Tenby who became a renowned mathematician and physician. Recorde's name may not be particularly well known but he was a Welshman who left the world a wonderful legacy, thanks to his groundbreaking work in his academic field, as well as proving competent in law, music and religion. He is often considered to have introduced algebra to Britain, in addition to creating the equals sign that has become an integral part of the subject in the modern era.

Recorde was born in the town shortly after the death of the first Tudor monarch Henry VII to a local family of reasonable wealth. An adolescent of great promise, Recorde was sent to Oxford University in 1525 at the age of fifteen, and six years later he was elected a Fellow of All Souls College. He also graduated from Cambridge in 1545 with a degree in medicine. Recorde also displayed his exceptionally academic nature in his mastering of Latin, Greek and French, in addition to English and possibly Welsh. Tragically for one of the most capable minds of the Tudor period he ended his days in a London debtor's prison under Queen Mary after entering a destructive conflict with one of her favourite courtiers, Sir William Herbert.

The marble plaque in the St Thomas Chapel proudly reads,

In memory of Robert Recorde, the eminent mathematician, who was born at Tenby, circa 1510. To his genius we owe the earliest important English treatises on algebra, arithmetic, astronomy and geometry: He also invented the sign of equality = now universally adopted by the civilised world.

Above this is an effigy allegedly of Recorde to add to the poignancy of the memorial to Tenby's most famous son.

Elsewhere in the chapel stands the inescapable tomb of the Whites, the aforementioned mayors of fifteenth-century Tenby, without whom there may never have been a Tudor dynasty. Tradition states that it was Mayor Thomas White and his son John who helped Jasper and Henry Tudor escape through the underground tunnels of Tenby during their evasion of pursuing Yorkists in 1471. Their town house was known to have been in close proximity to St Mary's, a position of noted prominence in the burgeoning merchant's town; it could even have been the present Jasperley House, which stands behind Boots. The Whites were wealthy and successful merchants in their own right, and Thomas and then John used their high-profile statuses to intermittently serve as mayors of the town throughout the late fifteenth century.

Situated next to each other, running parallel to the altar steps, the two alabaster tombs are conspicuous in their magnificence, perhaps unexpected of a regional parish church and clearly indicative of their importance in the town's history. The effigies atop the tomb portray father and son in long garments, which were typical of the late fifteenth century, with both men depicted with their hands on their chest in a praying manner. The Latin inscription on Thomas's tomb states that he died in 1482, while the corresponding engraving on his son's tomb has been lost, although sources state he passed away around 1507. The tombs also commemorate the wives of the Whites, with Thomas's sarcophagus listing his first wife Johana Howel and second wife Isabella Butler, along with his daughter-in-law Margaret Phillips. These same women are also illustrated in various carvings on the face of the tomb, with several depictions of the two generations along with their heraldic shields, a boastful display of their dynastic success during the early years of the Tudor era.

Elsewhere in the church can be found another tomb, this time a grisly depiction of an unknown cleric; it is commonly reputed to be that of Thomas Danby, a local priest known to be an acquaintance of Jasper Tudor and the Whites. It is possible Danby was also a collaborator in the Tudors' fortuitous escape in 1471. The effigy is contrasting to the Whites', depicting the priest as a decomposed cadaver, a decayed and emaciated corpse, as was occasionally the style of various religious figures of the medieval period.

St Mary's parish church is an ecclesiastical wonder of West Wales, and its spectacular spire often features as a remarkable backdrop to the traditional viewing of Tenby's Georgian exterior from the town's many delightful beaches. As a resort which sells itself on these beaches and the seaside in general, the church is often merely a structure the impatient visitor trudges past on their way to the shore. Inside St Mary's, however, is an often overlooked plethora of early Tudor attractions, which offer a suitably exquisite insight into Tenby's exciting past as an important fifteenth- and sixteenth-century settlement.

Cadaver tomb, St Mary's church.

Tenby Tudor Merchant's House

The National Trust-controlled Tudor Merchant's House is one of the top sixteenth-century places to visit in the United Kingdom, and insightfully portrays the life of a successful commercial family from around the year 1500, furnished and decorated in the burgeoning Renaissance style of the period. As it is a living museum, its volunteers can often be found in full Tudor costume, educating the visitor on the various tools a merchant family used in their day-to-day life and providing a unique and hands-on environment of learning in South Wales's best-preserved medieval building.

Tenby and its merchants were particularly fortunate that the naturally sheltered harbour lay on a section of water then known as the Severn Sea, a prime trading channel from which it was able to benefit greatly. By far the largest settlement within proximity of the sea was Bristol, a flourishing town developed upon the sea trade and often vying with York to be considered England's most important medieval town outside of London. The prominence of Bristol's involvement in the sea trade was such that the Severn Sea became known as the Bristol Channel, a name it has retained to the modern day, although in Welsh it is still known as Môr Hafren, the Severn Sea.

Tenby benefited from its proximity to Bristol, as the town was able to attract both importers and exporters along this busy oceanic thoroughfare. By 1500 the town's economy was thriving. A prime example of a merchant family achieving a degree of success in such conditions was the White family, wealthy multigenerational businessmen who provided the town with several mayors during the fifteenth century. Thomas White was in a position to allow the fleeing Tudors to requisition his barque in 1471, suggesting he had accumulated enough wealth from his profession to allow one of his larger ships to be taken without reservation.

Tenby underwent great architectural renovation in the Georgian and Victorian ages, with the inevitable destruction of the merchant dwellings from which the fifteenth- and sixteenth-century townspeople made their living. The Tudor Merchant's House, which remains standing on Bridge Street, is the sole survivor of the period, and as such is of significant historical importance to both the academic and the tourist. The three-storey building is nestled in tightly between Tudor Square and Crackwell Street, which allowed the owner easy access to the centre of town and the harbour via Quay Hill, an ideal setting from which to conduct his daily business. It was rescued from further deterioration by the National Trust over seventy-five years ago and restored to how the interior and exterior would have appeared in 1500, fifteen years into the Tudor reign.

The ground floor of the stone building would have been the most important in the house, for it was from this room that the merchant and his family made their living and funded their lifestyle. In effect this floor was transformed into his shop, and would have opened out into the street to entice passers-by into spending their money on his products. From this position the merchant would sell any goods he was able to import from the harbour, including wool, herbs and spices, and sugar. Salt imported from the Bay of

Biscay was also a much sought-after commodity, not only for its use as a table condiment but also due to its qualities in preserving meat and fish, an absolute necessity for the local people. The wine trade also enjoyed brisk business through the importing of tuns from Gascony in southern France.

The floor today reflects this hectic period, with various spices scattered atop the tables, and barrels stacked upon one another in the corner. The adjoining kitchen area has a great fireplace and would have been considered the beating heart of the household. The fireplace was core to the survival of the household, used to cook meats and fish, bake bread and provide warmth to the family. Its importance was demonstrated by the fact that it was generally kept burning twenty-four hours a day. Elsewhere in the room it's possible to view the various kitchen utensils the servants would have used, while learning about the different methods of cooking meats and herbs. Next to the fireplace is the opening from the latrine on the higher floors, which was also utilised to dispose of kitchen waste. At night, apple wood was added to the fire, as well as branches of pine and juniper, in order to help mask the unpleasant odours that undoubtedly emanated from the latrine opening.

The first floor presents the main living space of the merchant family – where they would have entertained both themselves and any visitors. Wall hangings and tapestries decorate the walls, adorned with various coats of arms and heraldic symbols displaying the family's political and religious affiliations. In the corner of the room beyond a curtain is the middle-floor latrine, while a lengthy table is situated in the middle of the room and holds various children's games, including musical instruments and chess. A wooden table and chair are situated in one part of the room with writing utensils and ink; perhaps this is where the merchant would spend his evenings composing letters and completing his accounts.

At the top end of the room is the head table, where the merchant and his wife would have sat facing the room during mealtimes, not unlike the dais that kings used at their royal palaces. The family would tend to break their fast around dawn with a meal which would typically involve pickled beef, cold meats and ale. Their main dinner was enjoyed before midday, and in a typical merchant's house this could consist of four or five courses. Other dishes enjoyed by the emerging merchant middle class were honey and cream flan, bacon soup, gingerbread and chicken in orange.

The second floor is home to the master bedroom of the merchant, replete with lavish tapestries and rugs surrounding a four-poster bed. A smaller fireplace in the corner of the room provided further warmth to the couple while they also enjoyed the use of their own private latrine. Two windows allowed a degree of light into the room during the daytime and also provided the merchant with a clear view of the harbour to witness his ships coming and going.

Tenby's Tudor Merchant's House is a rarity, in that it allows the visitor not just to read about the lives of the working classes but to see in person precisely how they existed. It's an invaluable educational tool, but also retains a degree of fun, needed to attract the casual visitor. It certainly is a museum that deserves higher recognition, and is worth visiting whenever in Tenby.

Tudor
Merchant's
House,
Tenby.

Cardiff Castle

Set in the heart of the Welsh capital, Cardiff Castle is often dismissed as a Victorian restoration project lacking medieval authenticity. In regards to part of the grounds this is certainly the case, but Cardiff Castle has been a functional fortress since the Roman age and has an intriguing medieval history, including a connection with the Tudor dynasty. A seat of various Norman Marcher Lords during the battle for regional supremacy with the Welsh in the twelfth and thirteenth centuries, the stronghold became the possession of the earls of Warwick in the 1400s. Richard III, then Duke of Gloucester, came into control of the Lordship of Cardiff in 1478, but upon his death at the Battle of Bosworth it came into the custody of the Crown, namely Henry Tudor, who in turn rewarded his loyal uncle, Jasper Tudor, with the property.

Jasper retained the castle and Lordship of Cardiff until his death in 1495 when the estate reverted to Crown control, and remained under the jurisdiction of Henry VII and his son Henry VIII for the entirety of their reigns. It was only in 1550 that the Tudors relinquished control of the castle, when King Edward VI granted possession to Sir William Herbert. Ironically Sir William's namesake grandfather, the great Earl of Pembroke, had been executed in 1469 at the Battle of Edgecote by the Kingmaker Richard Neville, the last Earl of Warwick to hold Cardiff Castle. The castle continued to be used as a prison during the Tudor era and was notable in 1542 for the execution of Thomas Capper, a local man who was burned as a heretic on the orders of King Henry VIII for espousing views judged to be sacrilegious. He is considered to be Wales's first Protestant martyr.

Although the Herbert family and subsequent owners would be responsible for the erection of an opulent mansion in the grounds, the towering Norman keep that would have been familiar to the sixteenth-century visitor still proudly stands atop the motte. Cardiff Castle may be renowned for its nineteenth-century renovation but this was once a fortress owned by four generations of Tudors, from Jasper Tudor to Edward VI. Also note the wonderful stained-glass windows depicting Jasper Tudor and Henrys VII and VIII in the Victorian main range.

Stained glass in Victorian range, Cardiff Castle.

Hay-on-Wye

Hay-on-Wye is renowned as the quaint 'town of books', and home to the Hay Book Festival, an annual soiree which draws visitors from around to globe to the small Mid Welsh border settlement. Due to its historically precarious position in the Welsh March, Hay-on-Wye both prospered and suffered during the medieval period, as generation upon generation of Welsh and English battled for regional supremacy. That being said, the town played no major role during the Tudor period; yet it does possess one sixteenth-century-related attraction of note. In 1995 a large white statue of King Henry VII was unveiled on the end wall of the old market hall, affording this inanimate Tudor monarch commanding views across Castle Square in a place of utmost prominence. The 6-foot figure is looking to his left while adorned with a crown upon his head, an orb in his left hand and a sceptre in his right hand. It is a portrayal of Henry Tudor in all his majestic glory, and currently the only one of its kind in Wales. The plaque below the statue proudly boasts, 'Henry VII first Welsh king of the English.'

Henry VII overlooking Hay-on-Wye.

Llandaff Cathedral

Llandaff Cathedral is the splendid seat of the Bishop of Llandaff and occupies a historic spot in the suburbs of Cardiff, its grand spire visible for many miles in spite of its low-lying position at the foot of a hill. Constructed on an ancient site of worship as far back as the sixth century, the cathedral was founded in the early twelfth century and was dedicated to saints Peter and Paul as well as the Welsh saints Dyfrid, Teilo and Euddogwy.

The cathedral suffered large-scale damage at the turn of the fifteenth century when it was attacked by the forces of Owain Glyndŵr, requiring a prolonged process of regeneration throughout the century. Part of this rebuilding occurred with the financial backing of Jasper Tudor, Earl of Pembroke and uncle to King Henry VII. After the accession of his nephew, Jasper was inundated with titles and lands, many of which were in south-east Wales, like the lordships of Cardiff and Glamorgan. Jasper was primarily responsible for subsidising the construction of the north-west tower, instantly identifiable even without the celebrated nineteenth-century spire. This generous endowment is recognised today in the tower's name: the Jasper Tower. The tower has a relatively simple base, consistent with the Gothic style of the late fifteenth century, and is crowned with four elaborate parapets. The third part of the stone tower now houses the bells, and ensures the Jasper Tower retains its integral place in the modern character of the cathedral. Elsewhere in the cathedral can be viewed a small and unobtrusive plaque dedicated to William Morgan, the renowned translator of the Bible into the Welsh language, who served as the Bishop of Llandaff from 1595 to 1601. The tablet reads, '*Llusern yw dy air i'm traed a llewyrch i'm llwybr,*' a translation of Psalm 119:105, which declares, 'Thy word is a lamp unto my feet, and a light unto my path.' Morgan's accomplishment was considered to have illuminated the word of God for the Welsh people, and is one of the greatest and most influential achievements in Welsh history.

Llandaff was regularly inundated with pilgrims eager to worship at the tomb of St Teilo, and after such practices were discouraged by the Reformation the cathedral suffered from lack of income. By 1590 the nave lay in a state of ruin, with only the Lady chapel accessible as a place of worship, a victim of the religious turmoil of the sixteenth century. It would be restored during the Victorian period.

Neath Abbey

The substantial ruins of Neath Abbey offer an insight into a turbulent era in Wales's religious history, with both pre- and post-Reformation remains in one location, giving the visitor an on-site education in the effects of the theological dispute. Founded in the twelfth century by the Normans and quickly developed by the Cistercian monks, the monastery rapidly attained great prestige and wealth, with lands not only in the Glamorgan area, but as far afield as Devon and Cornwall. The tranquillity of the abbey and its monks was harshly disturbed in 1539 when it was dissolved under the command of Thomas Cromwell, passing into the ownership of his nephew Sir Richard Williams three years later.

From this period, extensive rebuilding took place on the abbey grounds to construct an opulent Tudor mansion, the ruins of which can be viewed in the south-eastern part of the site, distinguishable because of the large rectangular windows typical of mid-sixteenth-century architecture. The cloisters in this part of the abbey had been part of the former monastery and were used in the conversion; a delightful vaulted chamber survived the rebuilding and was probably incorporated in the new mansion as a servants' hall or store room.

The Tudor mansion was abandoned in the seventeenth century, and today the ruins come under the guise of Neath Abbey, but when one enters the site it becomes abundantly clear that you are in the midst of two different structures: namely the former abbey and the mansion that replaced it after the Dissolution. It is a rewarding site and allows the visitor to observe the upheaval of the Reformation in person. Even today the ruins live up to their description by the great Tudor antiquary John Leland as 'the fairest abbey of all Wales'.

Opposite page: Jasper Tower, Llandaff Cathedral.

Above left: The Tudor house at Neath Abbey.

Above right: The ruins of Neath Abbey.

Newport Cathedral

St Woolos Cathedral, the anglicised name for Saint Gwynllyw, stands on Stow Hill overlooking the modern city, and provides the few existing Tudor links that can be attributed to Wales's third-largest city. Although heavily restored and perhaps not as outwardly opulent as other cathedrals, two tombs and a headless statue make a visit to St Woolos worthwhile for the Tudor enthusiast. High on the tower above the doorway stands an oddly captivating decapitated statue, which is presumed to be that of a former benefactor. It is generally acknowledged to be Jasper Tudor, Earl of Pembroke, Duke of Bedford and protective uncle to King Henry VII. Jasper was known to have helped fund the rebuilding of the parish church after it had been comprehensively destroyed by the forces of his distant kinsman Owain Glyndŵr in his sacking of Newport in 1402. The tower is still known today as the Jasper Tower, and the existence of Tudor rose ornamentation on the outer wall lends credence to this theory.

Inside the cathedral there are two tombs from the Tudor era. The first is the damaged remains of the sarcophagus of Sir John Morgan of Tredegar, a member of the local gentry who died in 1493. A renowned scion of a prominent local family during the instability of the Wars of the Roses, Morgan made an inspired decision to join the side of the Lancastrian claimant Henry Tudor shortly after his landing in West Wales in August 1485. Henry's force was conspicuously short of any Welsh nobles of note and Morgan was among the first to declare his intention to support Tudor's claim to the throne, joining with the main army at Cardigan on its march through Wales towards Bosworth.

His loyalty was rewarded when he was knighted in Henry's first parliament and made Steward of Machen, Sheriff of Gwenllwg and Newport, and Constable of Newport Castle. It was an ample display of gratitude from the new king to Morgan for his military assistance at a point when Tudor's forces were vulnerable. The tomb has mostly been lost, save for a portion; the plaque erected above the alabaster remains, stating,

> These fragments of alabaster are the only remains of a monument which once stood in the body of the church erected as the arms denote to the memory of Sir John Morgan of Tredegar Knight of the Holy Sepulchre who died 1493 and his wife Janet daughter and heiress of David Mathew of Llandaff esquire.

The second tomb in St Woolos is that of Sir Walter Herbert of St Julian's, which is situated at the back of the south aisle, erected in memoriam to a grandson of the great Sir William Herbert, Yorkist Earl of Pembroke in the 1460s. A consistent presence in local governance throughout his life, including a stint as deputy steward to Henry Somerset, Earl of Worcester, Walter was knighted in 1549 and served as High Sheriff of Monmouthshire the following year. He never finished this term, dying while still in office, and being replaced by his son. The Renaissance tomb he was interred in is heavily weathered, but still remains a remarkable effigy to the head of this junior branch of the mighty Herbert family.

Above: Jasper Tudor statue, Newport Cathedral.

Right: Tomb of Sir Walter Herbert, Newport Cathedral.

Old Beaupre Castle

Technically a fortified manor house rather than a castle, after its remodelling into a Tudor mansion, Old Beaupre was originally built in the fourteenth century just outside the village of St Hilary in the Vale of Glamorgan, a country home for prominent members of the local gentry. The name Beaupre was derived from the Norman-French for beautiful retreat, and neatly sums up the setting for this Tudor home. Much of the site is ruined, although the gatehouse and porch remain well preserved, with a degree of atmospheric authenticity due to the lack of modernisation in the immediate area, save for the farmyard equipment in the adjoining building.

Standing on private land and not marketed as a tourist attraction, Old Beaupre is a deserted location in picturesque surroundings, which, being relatively unchanged since the 1500s, gives the visitor an unspoilt glimpse into the views enjoyed by the Tudor-era inhabitants of the manor house. Access to the site is via a public footpath across three fields from a country lane, an atmospheric approach to this wonderful castle.

The Tudor remodelling commenced under the ownership of courtier Sir Rice Mansel in the middle of the sixteenth century, before being continued by the Basset family. It was during these periods of renovation that the outer gatehouse and west lodgings were built, while in 1600 the exceptionally carved Renaissance porch, complete with Tudor arch, was added. The porch is a true wonder of late Tudor architecture yet is regrettably little known due to the site's low-key status. The three-storey entranceway was designed in the Greek fashion, and prominent on the second level is the Basset family coat of arms, a display of pride also replicated on the outer gatehouse. The lodgings, meanwhile, still provide evidence of a lavish fireplace, while a Tudor rose can be viewed, carved above another fireplace in the cordoned-off upper drawing room. Old Beaupre is certainly worth tracking down, as the atmospheric ruins are substantial, although sadly much of the inner castle is now inaccessible due to health and safety considerations.

Oxwich Castle

The Gower Peninsula is regularly cited as one of the most picturesque areas in Western Europe and it is unsurprising that these scenic environs served as the backdrop to various manor houses in the fifteenth and sixteenth centuries. As at Sir Rhys ap Thomas's Weobley in the north of the peninsula, Oxwich Castle served as the home of another prosperous Welsh family that enjoyed greater status under the Tudor sovereigns, namely the Mansels.

Constructed in close proximity to the bay and Oxwich Wood, the castle first appears to have been inhabited by Philip Mansel in 1459, before its later redevelopment from stronghold to fortified manor house under his descendants Sir Rice and Edward Mansel. Sir Rice Mansel was a competent soldier, sailor and administrator, who was born two years into the reign of King Henry VII, a fortunate time for an ambitious Welshman to prosper and something Sir Rice took advantage of once he reached adulthood. Although he achieved a degree of local importance during the reign of Henry VIII, it was under the rule of Henry's daughter Mary that his career reached its pinnacle, with an appointment to the chancellorship of South Wales and a royal licence to keep a retinue of fifty gentlemen.

Situated on a headland overlooking the modern settlement, Oxwich Castle retains substantial ruins of the rebuilding, and demonstrates the layout of this manor house at its Tudor peak. Entered through a gateway emblazoned with the coat of arms of Sir Rice, it is immediately evident that the castle's main living quarters were constructed beyond the sizable outer courtyard, as was typical of the period. The first building encountered on the right-hand side is Sir Rice's modest southern block, built between 1520 and 1538, here he and his young family resided before their later rise in favour prompted a move to Margam.

The castle was extended after Sir Rice's death in 1559 by his son Edward, who proceeded on an extensive building programme which may have contributed to his later financial difficulties. Edward's East Range is conspicuous by its towering height in comparison to the diminished southern block, its formidable outer wall rendered more so by the destruction of the porch, which at one time offered a gateway to the first-floor hall. Built by Edward sometime between 1559 and 1580, this East Range offered far more opulent residential quarters for the Mansels and their household, the centrepiece of which was the hall and the lengthy Elizabethan gallery, which occupied the second floor. The remains of the large window at the end of the gallery are still evident.

The astonishing South West Tower still displays the six floors that originally made it such an imposing addition to the castle, with windows and fireplaces on each level suggesting that the tower provided accommodation to a large number of people, much like a modern high-rise dwelling. Constructed at the same time was the dovecot, still standing half-destroyed outside the East Range. Although it no longer possesses its domed roof, the many nesting holes can still be viewed, and this bird store would have played an integral part in supplying the household with eggs and meat. Oxwich is an authentic Tudor mansion, and provides an insight into how a family developed their property to accompany their rise in society; at Oxwich, this progression is exhibited through the architectural differences between the South Block and the East Range.

Raglan Castle

Raglan Castle is a grandiose ruin close to the English border in Monmouthshire, and must be considered among the finest such examples in the country. The spectacularly unique gatehouse and colossal Great Keep ensure that Raglan is a worthy place to visit – it has no doubt been an attraction since the fifteenth century. Described by Thomas Churchyard in 1587 as a 'rare and noble sight', Raglan enjoys a peculiar claim to fame in that it was the childhood home of the first Tudor king, Henry VII, who was placed here as a four-year-old boy in 1461.

Raglan was primarily noted as the base of the powerful Herbert family, a clan of Welsh nobles who were the fifteenth-century rivals to the Tudors throughout the turbulent Wars of the Roses, with both families seeking supremacy within Wales for their respective leaders. The fortress's position in the Marcher lands of south-east Wales warranted the castle a degree of prestige as a good conduit between rural West Wales and the industrious citadel that was London; thus, it was an ideal location for the Herbert family to solidify their political and commercial interests.

Although a castle had long stood on the site, Raglan first gained wider prominence under Sir William ap Thomas, a veteran of the Battle of Agincourt in 1415, and it was he who began to dramatically improve the amenities and structure of the property. A conspicuous feature of Sir William's home was the French-style great tower, a five-storey hexagonal keep with an innovative design that was effectively an alien concept in fifteenth-century England. The so-called Tower of Gwent is an imposing structure as a ruin, but must have been a colossus during its prime, and served as a distinguishing feature of Raglan, designed to awe the visitor. Although severely ruined, it is possible to view each floor from outside the structure, and observe the differing functions of each level from the basement kitchen to the apartments above.

The castle would pass into the control of Sir William's son William Herbert, who continued his father's renovations to make Raglan an even greater display of wealth and status, particularly as he climbed the social ladder to become one of the pre-eminent magnates of the mid-fifteenth century. Herbert was a renowned Yorkist during the internecine conflict between the rival claimants for the English throne in the 1450s, and through his diligent adherence to the White Rose he enjoyed an abundance of authority when his patron Edward of March became king in 1461. He became the first Welshman to enter the English peerage when he was made Lord Herbert of Raglan in 1461 and promoted even further to Earl of Pembroke in 1468, satisfactorily replacing his attainted rival Jasper Tudor in the process. Herbert was also made Justice and Chamberlain of South Wales, and gained the privileged distinction of becoming an integral part of the king's inner circle.

It is of no surprise to learn that Herbert resolved to drastically improve Raglan Castle to reflect the fact that he was a powerful magnate. His most opulent addition was the aforementioned Great Gatehouse, which was added around 1460, consisting of an entranceway dividing two half-hexagonal towers. Particularly notable are the machicolations that adorn the top of the gatehouse; they are a series of arched openings

The Great Gatehouse, Raglan Castle.

Elizabethan Great Hall, Raglan Castle.

which not only offered defence in the event of a siege, but also added an element of grandeur to the entranceway. These openings in the battlement level were designed so that objects such as rocks and stones could be dropped on attackers during a siege. The passageway in between the domineering gatehouse towers would have possessed two portcullises, which added a further level of defence to Herbert's castle, although the wooden drawbridge over the moat has since been changed to a permanent stone feature.

Inside the gatehouse can be seen sixteenth-century modifications such as the Tudor fireplaces, while the exterior, which overlooks the Pitched Stone Court, displays the elaborate window frames of Herbert's first-floor gallery. The ruined Office Wing on the north-eastern side was rebuilt during the Tudor period, while at the end stands the hexagonal kitchen tower, complete with two large fireplaces, which would have been used to prepare the food for Herbert's court, including young Henry Tudor. Herbert was also responsible for extending the lavish Great Hall, although the great oriel window was a later addition by the 3rd Earl of Somerset.

In addition, Herbert was instrumental in the alterations to the fine Fountain Court, including the wonderful Great Stair, which would have offered access to a series of apartments for the Herbert family and guests, including Henry Tudor during the 1460s. Herbert's additions ensured that Raglan had been transformed within a generation from a medieval border stronghold into one of the most comfortable stately homes, suitable as the home of one of the pre-eminent courtiers of the age, with advantageous views north-west towards the Brecon Beacons.

As the Herberts rose, the Tudors fell. The enmity between the two parties had intensified after the Herbert affinity attacked Edmund Tudor at Carmarthen Castle in 1456, an action that probably led to the Earl of Richmond's early death after his imprisonment at Herbert's hands. It might be argued that the hatred went further – back to Owain Glyndŵr's Welsh War of Independence, when Herbert's grandfather, Dafydd Gam, and the Penmynydd Tudurs were politically opposed. The feud reached an irrevocable level after the Battle of Mortimer's Cross in 1461 when Herbert's Yorkists defeated Jasper Tudor's Lancastrians. Owen Tudor, father of Jasper and grandfather of Henry, was captured by Herbert's half-brother Roger Vaughan and executed in Hereford. Jasper was forced to flee the country and leave behind his young nephew at Pembroke Castle. Both the castle and the child were shortly captured by Herbert, and Henry Tudor's wardship briefly reverted to the Crown before Sir William purchased the rights and moved the four-year-old to Raglan. Henry would spend the next decade living with the Herbert family.

At Raglan, young Henry would come under the control of Herbert's wife Anne Devereux and was brought up as an integral part of the noble household. Men rating among the very best tutors were assigned to him – namely Edward Haseley and Andrew Scot, two graduates from Oxford University – in order to provide the young master with a top education. Sir Hugh Johns of Gower was also noted to have instructed Henry in military matters. Bernard André would later record in his biased but detailed biography of his patron King Henry VII that 'after he reached the age of understanding, he was handed over to the best and most upright instructors to be taught the first principles of literature'.

Henry must have been a willing student and a keen learner, for he was also recorded as being endowed with such sharp mental powers and such great natural vigour and comprehension that even as a young boy he learned everything pertaining to religious instruction rapidly and thoroughly, with little effort from his teachers. Indeed, at this time the highest disposition for virtue shone forth in the boy, and he was so attentive in reading and listening to the divine office that all who watched him saw signs of his future goodness and success. When as a young man he was initiated into the first principles of literature, he surpassed his peers with the same quick intellect he had displayed as a boy.

When Henry became king, he displayed his gratitude to what must have been a fulfilling education when he rewarded those who had played a part in his childhood. When Polydore Vergil created his biography of Henry he recorded of the king's early years that he was 'kept as a prisoner, but honourably brought up'. To this effect the king brought Anne Devereux to court once he was crowned to show favour and deference to the woman who had played a key part in his development. Sir William Herbert was executed in 1469 after the Battle of Edgecote, and Raglan eventually fell into the hands of his younger son Sir Walter Herbert, a childhood acquaintance of Henry Tudor, who had switched sides from York to Lancastrian before the Battle of Bosworth in 1485. Sir Walter and Raglan played host to Queen Elizabeth of York in 1502, as she visited the castle which had not only been the childhood home of her husband but also the home of her aunt Mary Woodville, wife to Sir William Herbert's eldest son William the younger.

The castle passed into the control of Sir Charles Somerset in 1508 through his marriage to heiress Elizabeth Herbert, and the Somerset family would retain ownership until the twentieth century. Sir Charles was a legitimised scion of the House of Beaufort, and his father Henry Beaufort and the king's mother Margaret Beaufort were first cousins, so the Somersets were among the king's closest relations. He also served as King Henry's Captain of the Yeoman of the Guard and Lord Chamberlain before being ennobled as the Earl of Worcester in 1514 under Henry VIII.

His grandson Sir William Somerset was a prominent courtier during the individual reigns of Henry VIII's three children, and was accountable for the final phase of building at Raglan, completing its transformation from medieval fortress to sixteenth-century home. Sir William rebuilt the Great Hall and added the sizable oriel window above the dais, which provided a large degree of light, while his weathered coat of arms is still visible on the southern wall. Somerset was also responsible for the addition of the multi-storey porch outside the hall and the great fireplace within, which would have provided warmth to his court while they feasted and enjoyed the festivities. The earl is also likely to have been accountable for the marble fountain which once stood in the centre of the Fountain Court and lent its name to the courtyard; only the base now remains where the opulent monument once stood.

Raglan Castle is a ruin, yet retains evidence of its former glory, allowing the visitor an insight into life at this stately home during the fifteenth and sixteenth centuries. During the childhood of Henry Tudor the castle had recently been transformed from stronghold to home and would have afforded the youth a pleasant upbringing despite his status as enforced ward of the man responsible for his father's death. It also provides sumptuous evidence of a Tudor-era palatial home under the successful Somerset dynasty, respected courtiers and kinsmen of the later Tudor monarchs.

Above: The Fountain Court, Raglan Castle.

Left: Elizabethan ornamentation, Raglan Castle.

Right: Tudor fireplaces, Raglan Castle.

Below: Ruins of the Tower of Gwent, Raglan Castle.

St Fagans National History Museum

St Fagans is a renowned open-air museum on the outskirts of Cardiff, and can truly be considered an icon of Wales, a site which by its very nature is rich in Tudor connections. Opened in 1948 and formerly known as the Museum of Welsh Life, the concept involves the restoration and preservation of historic Welsh buildings within the museum grounds for future generations. The exhibitions cover a wide period of history over the last 1,500 years, including an intriguing collection of structures focused on the Tudor period.

The most recent addition is the Pembrokeshire Tudor trader's house, a structure which originally stood in the once prosperous Quay Street in Haverfordwest before its dismantling in the 1980s. Arduously rebuilt brick by brick in 2012, the trader's house has been designed to appear as it would have done in 1580 at the height of the Elizabethan period. Not dissimilar to the National Trust's merchant's house in Tenby, the St Fagans interpretation offers the visitor the opportunity to learn how the occupiers of the house would have made their living – through sea and land trade, dealing in such goods as wool, salt, fish and wine. It is also possible to experience the single room above the ground floor, which would have been the living quarters of the family, complete with a fireplace and garderobe.

St Teilo's church is another location within St Fagans which has been redeveloped to appear as it would have done during the rule of the Tudors, in this case around the year 1520 and pre-Reformation. Constructed at various periods from the late twelfth century and originally located in Llandeilo Tal-y-Bont near Pontarddulais, St Teilo's is a late medieval Catholic church from a period when such places were about to come under threat by the Protestant reformers; it is complete with brightly coloured wall paintings and carvings typical of Catholic churches in the 1520s. Also notable is the wooden rood screen, a feature which generally disappeared from parish churches once the Reformation was complete.

Completing St Fagans' Tudor-themed collection is the Garreg Fawr farmhouse, originally built in 1544, and the Hendre'r-ywydd Uchaf farmhouse, which was built in 1508. Hendre'r-ywydd is a typical late medieval hall-house with timber-framed walls and a thatched roof; it was relocated from Denbighshire. Garreg Fawr, originally based in Waunfawr in Gwynedd, was once the home of a prosperous farming family. St Fagans has an abundance of historically intriguing exhibitions, each building offering a fascinating insight into our past. The Tudor-era structures are no different, and certainly help educate the visitor on how the average man existed in the often unforgiving and uncertain sixteenth-century world.

Pembroke trader's house, St Fagans.

Interior of St Teilo's church, St Fagans.

Weobley Castle

Weobley Castle is an obscure but outstanding medieval structure built on the north coast of the Gower Peninsula, and will certainly remain ingrained in the consciousness of all who visit it. While it can certainly be argued that Weobley is a castle in the traditional sense, it is perhaps more accurate to consider it as a fortified manor house, a pleasant rural retreat, as opposed to a military stronghold. Weobley's evocative location high above the Loughor Estuary affords the visitor a sensational view across the Llanrhidian marshlands below, the panorama from the castle appearing the same as it did over 500 years ago during the ownership of Sir Rhys ap Thomas, Henrys VII and VIII's trusted lieutenant in South Wales.

Built in the thirteenth century by the de la Bere family before the tenancy of Sir Rhys, the splendour of the manor house can still be determined in the existing ruins of the windows, garderobes and fireplaces; Weobley was evidently a comfortable place for the nobleman to relax. Sir Rhys is credited with the addition of the two-storey porch block in around 1500; this would have ensured a stately entrance to the Great Hall and private quarters, and served as an ostentatious show of wealth similar to what he ordered at his residence in Carew. Once inside Sir Rhys's porch, the small stairway takes you into the heart of his plush retreat, with a small chamber immediately ahead, with two sculpted windows and a sizable fireplace providing comfort to the occupier. The chimney on the east side of the porch was also built around this period – further indication of the building's transformation from castle to country house. In the exhibition hall, which once served as the lord's solar, note the latrine passage which stands in the corner of the room, a practical inclusion which afforded guests a degree of privacy without the need to leave the lavish confines of the solar.

The property passed into the control of Sir Rhys's daughter-in-law Catherine Edgecumbe after her son Gruffydd ap Rhys was executed in 1531 for treason. After her death, her son's attainder was activated and the property was repossessed by the Crown, before being leased to Sir William Herbert and then the Mansel family of Gower. Today the manor house stands as an example of the peace that came to Wales after the accession of the Tudors, showing the preference for a comfortable country retreat as opposed to a domineering but impractical fortress.

Tŷ Gwyn, Barmouth

During the 1460s the small, sleepy seaside village of Barmouth played an integral role in the intrigues and conspiracies of the Wars of the Roses, machinations led by the Welsh Lancastrian commander Jasper Tudor. As Harlech was the only fortress left under secure Lancastrian control after 1461, it was imperative for Jasper to maintain regular contact with the impregnable stronghold, and, due to its position roughly 10 miles south of the castle, Barmouth found itself dragged into the conflict.

The erstwhile Earl of Pembroke's base was Tŷ Gwyn, a sturdy structure that stands overlooking the rough waters of Cardigan Bay, allowing him convenient access to and from the sea while eluding capture by his enemies. Its nearness to the sea was captured in prose by contemporary poet Tudur Penllyn, who described Tŷ Gwyn as the 'house built in the waves'. Tŷ Gwyn, which means White House, was built by a local devotee of Jasper Tudor called Gruffydd Fychan of nearby Cors y Gedol; he was a respected local member of the community, and constructed the convenient building at the beginning of the decade as a meeting point for exiled Lancastrians.

The timber roof is now restored and houses a bustling restaurant and shipwreck museum. The building is still in close proximity to the sea, although it is now surrounded by the urbanisation of a modern seaside resort. Nonetheless it is possible to picture this quaint little stone building as it appeared during the fifteenth and sixteenth centuries when it was one of only a couple of houses in the area, and was continually battered by the rough winter sea. It served Jasper Tudor well and enabled him to plot resolutely the restoration of his family from exiles to royalty.

Tŷ Gwyn overlooking the sea.

Beaumaris Castle

Beaumaris is a historic town situated on the south-east coast of Anglesey facing the Menai Strait, with Snowdonia providing an exquisite backdrop. The town developed around the castle, which was commissioned by Edward I in 1295 as part of the king's policy to subdue the native population after the completion of his brutal conquest of Wales. Built in a concentric style – it is often regarded to be the finest example in existence of such an architectural design – the castle today is a World Heritage Site, along with Edward's other North Wales constructions. In March 1382 the local nobleman, Goronwy ap Tudur, was appointed the castle's constable, an unusual appointment as no Welshman had been inserted into such an authoritative position in the castle's eighty-seven-year history.

Although he died only four days later by mysteriously drowning in a Kentish port, the appointment itself was innovative in its application, demonstrating not only a temporary softening in attitude to the Welsh but also the exalted reputation afforded to this respected member of the local community. His brother Rhys ap Tudur also came into territorial control of the castle after Goronwy's death; he was appointed an official of Dindaethwy, which included the town of Beaumaris. Their link to the royal Tudor dynasty was through their youngest brother Maredudd ap Tudur, great-grandfather of the first Tudor monarch, King Henry VII. Rhys would turn against the English Crown in 1400 and ally himself with his cousin Owain Glyndŵr, an alliance which naturally incurred the forfeiture of the Tudors' position of power at Beaumaris. In one notable episode, Rhys's force in Anglesey caused a mortified King Henry IV to flee to the safety of Beaumaris, an act which earned the Tudors the enmity of the English king.

By the sixteenth century the castle was in dire need of financial restoration but, if some circumstantial accounts are to be believed, it once more came under the direct control of the Tudor family in 1509, when Sir Roland de Velville was unexpectedly appointed constable by King Henry VIII. This mysterious Breton had arrived in England in 1485 as a member of Henry Tudor's invasion force, and would remain loyal to the Tudor regime for the rest of his life, earning a knighthood in 1497 along with many other rewards. The novelty of his continued favour with the Tudors has led to a belief that Sir Roland was in fact an illegitimate son of Henry Tudor from Henry's time spent in exile in Brittany. This belief is lent credence by Velville's appointment to lands and estates in North Wales, which at one time belonged to the Tudors, particularly considering that the Breton had no obvious link to the region himself.

Beaumaris Castle is a fantastically atmospheric fortress, and played an important part in further solidifying the Tudor family's status in North Wales in the late fourteenth century. Its concentric design can be pleasantly confusing to navigate, while allowing one to understand the provincial significance this large castle must have had in the medieval period. Beaumaris may not have the strongest links to the Tudors in North Wales, but nonetheless it has played an integral role in further advancing the

family's standing in their locality, a reputation that was rapidly destroyed by their involvement in the Welsh Wars of Independence under their kinsman Glyndŵr. For this reason the castle is an intriguing place to visit, as the location where the Tudors arguably reached their zenith in the fourteenth century with their appointments in the town.

Previous page: Beaumaris Castle gatehouse.

Below: The concentric walls of Beaumaris Castle.

Beaumaris Castle and moat.

Beaumaris Castle gatehouse.

Chirk Castle

Chirk Castle enjoys a commanding hilltop position on the Welsh–English border and is notable for its continuous state of residential occupation, which lasted almost seven centuries. It was built by the powerful magnate Roger Mortimer shortly after the Norman conquest of Wales in the late thirteenth century and has been utilised ever since, both as fortress and stately home.

The modern castle retains a medieval charm on the exterior, while the interior has undergone varying degrees of renovation over the last few hundred years that has ensured it is no longer recognisable as a medieval or Tudor home. Nonetheless, while the castle may be lacking in authentic Tudor furnishings, it does still enjoy strong links with the dynasty, which ensures it remains a worthwhile location to visit.

From 1439 to 1464 the castle was in the possession of the Beaufort family, the maternal relations of Henry Tudor through his mother Margaret Beaufort. The property had been purchased by the dominant Cardinal Henry Beaufort and in turn passed to his nephew Edmund Beaufort, 2nd Duke of Somerset, and his son Henry, 3rd Duke of Somerset. Both Beaufort dukes were integral parts of the Lancastrian faction during the Wars of the Roses, and contemporaries of Jasper Tudor during the internecine conflict, and both would be killed by their Yorkist adversaries. After the destruction of the Beauforts, the castle passed into the brief control of Richard, Duke of Gloucester, the future Richard III, before finding its way to Sir William Stanley. Fittingly, the property would eventually find its way back into Beaufort hands when it was judicially seized by Henry Tudor from Stanley, whom the king executed for treason in 1495. It would remain in the ownership of the Tudors until 1563.

While the interior of the castle is of a later period and the majority of the exterior from the fourteenth and fifteenth centuries, the south range is known to have been constructed during the Tudor ownership, and was rebuilt in 1529 on behalf of Henry VIII. Queen Elizabeth I eventually granted Chirk to Robert Dudley in 1563 and the Earl of Leicester held it until his death in 1588. Seven years later it was purchased for the substantial sum of £5,000 by Sir Thomas Myddleton, a successful London-based merchant who was a co-founder of the East India Company and a wealthy associate of Drake, Raleigh and Hawkins. Sir Thomas would be responsible for completing the castle's transformation from medieval castle to stately home, and the property has remained in his family until the present day.

Conwy Castle

Conwy Castle was the scene of a daring Tudor raid on 1 April 1401 when the Tudurs of Penmynydd, a troop of brothers who had been prominent officials in the region under English rule, attacked and seized the royal fortress on the north coast of Wales. The capture was organised by Rhys and Gwilym ap Tudur in conjunction with their cousin Owain Glyndŵr's uprising elsewhere in North Wales; their younger brother Maredudd, great-grandfather to the future King Henry VII, may also have been involved. The Tudur brothers proceeded to bring financial ruin to the castle, and burnt the town that stood within its walls, causing great anger and embarrassment to the English authorities, as the fortress had been built solely to enforce the subjugation of the local Welsh. The castle was eventually surrendered, but the Tudurs' audacious role in the Glyndŵr rebellion would long be recounted as a great Welsh tactical victory.

Today the World Heritage Site is one of North Wales's premier tourist attractions and is noted for its imposing position on a rock overlooking the Conwy estuary. The castle consists of an inner and outer ward protected by eight looming towers and a drawbridge leading to the West Barbican gate. Its sheer size serves to reinforce the bold and risky strategy of the Tudur brothers in attacking, and the improbability of their success in capturing a castle that was designed to withstand any prolonged siege.

Conwy Castle gatehouse.

Plas Mawr, Conwy

Situated in the heart of the historic castle town of Conwy, Plas Mawr mansion stands proudly conspicuous among the wealth of modern shops and public houses that line the crowded high street, a remnant of the town's prosperous sixteenth-century past. Plas Mawr, meaning 'Great Hall', was built between 1576 and 1585 by local merchant Robert Wynn, and today his Elizabethan construction remains one of the finest surviving town houses of the period anywhere in Britain.

Wynn was an affluent trader who had succeeded in amassing a respectable fortune from importing various products. As was typical of the flourishing merchant class, he invested his earnings in an opulent display of newfound status in the form of a lavish manorial home. He had risen to become a distinguished member of the Welsh gentry, and desired to exhibit this to the community, hence the development of Plas Mawr. Wynn pronounced his project to be a 'worthy, plentiful house' and this description is as true today as it was during the late sixteenth century.

Wynn was the third son of John Wynn ap Meredith, titular head of the former royal House of Aberffraw, and as such suffered from minimal inheritance in favour of his elder siblings. This certainly played a part in Robert travelling extensively throughout Europe during the reign of King Henry VIII, and this period would undoubtedly influence both his business practices and architectural preferences upon his belated return to Conwy. Wynn had been wounded in the leg during Henry VIII's siege of Boulogne in 1544 and also served during the Scottish campaign later that year. After such excitement it is no surprise that the adventurer would seek out a calmer existence at home and use the wealth he had built up during these eventful years to cement his position in the regional ruling class, establishing his own family in the process. From his extravagant Plas Mawr base Wynn was appointed a justice of the peace in 1575 and 1581, an MP for Caernarvonshire in 1589 and sheriff in the region from 1590 to 1591. He died in 1598 and was buried in the nearby St Mary's church; his legacy to Conwy remains, over 400 years later, in the enduring structure of Plas Mawr.

Wynn purchased the property in 1570 and, after acquiring further land, six years later began his reconstruction of Plas Mawr. The north range was built first, and contained a brewhouse and parlour on the ground floor with two bedrooms on the first floor. The chamber that stands over the brewhouse is considered to have been the private room of Robert Wynn, and unsurprisingly contains elaborate plasterwork which details his lineage in an ostentatious attempt to display his pedigree. Among the various decorations is the eagle emblem of Wynn's prestigious ancestor Owain Gwynedd, with the Tudor rose and fleur-de-lis also noticeable. Prominent over the fireplace is the Wynn coat of arms, with Robert's initials 'RG' leaving the visitor in no doubt as to whom this chamber belonged to.

In 1580 Wynn's second phase of building was completed when he added the central and southern ranges, which housed the buttery, kitchen and pantry on the ground floor with the great chamber above. The chamber room has been redecorated in its original colours and contains an ornate homage to Queen Elizabeth I in the form of a large Tudor rose, enclosed between her regal initials ER, above the fireplace. Once more the Wynn coat of arms appears on the roof while the Tudor rose is displayed in abundance on the wall tapestries. It is a recurring theme throughout Plas Mawr that symbols relating to the Tudor dynasty can be found next to Wynn's own coat of arms, a demonstration of the merchant's pride in both his own pedigree and that of his sovereign. The intricate detail of the friezes fails to disguise the money Wynn must have spent on this rich interior, with no expense being spared to impress any visitors.

Wynn's great rebuilding work was finally completed in 1585 when he succeeded in his acquisition of a plot of land which faced High Street. This allowed him to build the great gatehouse, which serves as the flamboyant façade to his unrivalled town house, and which certainly impresses the passer-by; undoubtedly, this was Wynn's intention. Noticeable on the exterior of the doorway is the Tudor coat of arms, resplendent with the Welsh dragon, while the gatehouse building consists of three floors as opposed to the standard two elsewhere in the complex. The first floor of this section includes a hall and chamber, which would have accommodated the steward of the household, while the second floor houses a sufficiently large gallery. It is an enormous structure in comparison with the modern erections which surround it, and stands proud as a symbol of Conwy's Tudor merchant past.

Elizabethan façade, Plas Mawr gatehouse.

Plas Mawr offers an authentic Tudor experience as one follows in the very footsteps of the people who succeeded in ensuring this magnificent mansion prospered in its historic North Welsh setting during the late sixteenth century. Whether you're exploring the great chambers, which housed members of the gentry, or braving the pantry and kitchen, in which the servants belonged, Plas Mawr is a true Tudor treasure, and ranks among the most impressive of such structures, not just in Wales but throughout the UK.

Also worth viewing at the end of High Street is Aberconwy House, a Tudor dwelling rebuilt on the existing foundations of an earlier medieval building. Although the interior of this National Trust building has been renovated, rather anachronistically, in the eighteenth- and nineteenth-century style, the exterior of the building retains its original character. Evident is the typical sixteenth-century external staircase leading to the first floor, as well as the worn timber framing, allowing the observer to enjoy a glimpse into Tudor Conwy away from Plas Mawr.

Above: Tudor coat of arms, Plas Mawr.

Opposite page: Denbigh Castle gatehouse.

Denbigh Castle

Resting high above the market town of Denbigh, this picturesque ruin has had a tumultuous history in a region often devastated in a series of vicious conflicts between Welsh and English, Yorkist and Lancastrian, and Royalist and Parliamentarian. Rebuilt in the thirteenth century by Edward I, Denbigh Castle has been on the front line of many clashes between opposing factions, and was both defended and attacked by Jasper Tudor during the Wars of the Roses.

The crumbling gatehouse still retains a degree of its former splendour and it is possible to visualise the grandness of this entranceway during the mid-fifteenth century. Denbigh Castle was strongly fortified with three octagonal towers, one of which still stands, albeit with significant damage. The castle was certainly a well-defended fortification that was difficult to capture. Its strategically important position in the north-east of Wales also ensured Denbigh Castle played a significant role in the Wars of the Roses, and in January 1460 King Henry VI granted the stronghold to his half-brother Jasper Tudor in order to subdue any burgeoning Yorkist sentiment in the region. Jasper was also bestowed with the Lordship of Denbigh in conjunction with the castle.

After the removal from the throne of Jasper's half-brother, and the accession of the Yorkists, the former Earl of Pembroke had been ousted from Denbigh, but he returned in 1468 in a vain attempt to retake his former possession. Jasper's efficient force relentlessly sacked the town and left the shattered settlement ablaze with flames. He caused such substantial ruin to Denbigh that a local rhyme existed about his exploits, '*Harddlech a Dinbech pob dor yn cynneu, Nan'conwy yn farwor, Mil pedwar cant oediant Ior, A thru'gain ac wyth ehagor*', which translates as 'In Harlech and Denbigh every door flaming, the Vale of Conway reduced to embers, in the year of our Lord 1468.'

The Lordship and castle of Denbigh later came under the control of Robert Dudley, Earl of Leicester and notorious favourite of Queen Elizabeth I, from 1563 until his death in 1588. He initiated plans to construct a large church in the grounds, and renovated the domestic apartments within the castle, while his son and heir Robert was styled Lord Denbigh until his tragic death at only four years old.

St Marcella's Church, Llanfarchell, Denbigh

St Marcella's is a charming parish church situated around a mile to the east of the town of Denbigh, near to where the hectic urban environment uneasily clashes with the rural quietness of the Denbighshire countryside. It served as a religious centre of worship for the Welsh citizens of the area before and during the medieval English settlement of the town. In spite of its curiously obscure location outside the town, albeit with envious views towards the rolling hills of the Clwydian range, the church has retained its importance and remained popular with worshippers since the turbulent Middle Ages, including the Tudor period.

Instantaneously identifiable as medieval due to the perpendicular style of construction and conspicuous whitewashed tower, which naturally earned the church the alternative name of Whitchurch, St Marcella's is notable as the resting place of a couple of regionally significant members of the Tudor gentry, who prospered during the Elizabethan period. The magnificent alabaster tomb which draws in the visitor is that of Sir John Salusbury, who died in 1578, and his wife Joan; it has effigies depicting the Elizabethan fashion of the late sixteenth century. Sir John was a scion of the Salusbury family, who had settled in the region shortly after the Norman Conquest and had begun to rise in social circles after the accession of Henry VII in 1485. Sir John's painted tomb lies in the erstwhile private chapel of the family and depicts its subject in armour complete with Elizabethan neck ruff, a sword and a hunting knife. The base of the tomb depicts their nine sons and four daughters, as well as the family coat of arms.

In the north chapel is a Victorian monument to Humphrey Llwyd, a noted Member of Parliament and cartographer who died in 1568. Llwyd, whose adage during life was '*hwy pery klod na golyd*', or 'fame lasts longer than wealth', is renowned for his work producing the first accurate maps of Wales, in addition to his work as a physician and musician – he was an acclaimed Renaissance man. A monumental brass dedicated to another contemporary can be found nearby affixed to the wall, portraying Richard Myddelton, his wife and his sixteen children, one of whom was Thomas Myddelton, later Lord Mayor of London. Elsewhere there is a depiction of a crowned female, which may represent Margaret Beaufort, great patroness of churches in this north-east corner of Wales.

Tomb of Sir John Salusbury, St Marcella's church.

St Marcella's church, Denbigh.

All Saints Church, Gresford

Gresford is the site of the impressive All Saints Church, a striking holy structure and one of the so-called Seven Wonders of Wales; it instantaneously exhibits a certain magnificence when viewed for the first time. The splendour of the church seems out of place for this small settlement on the Welsh border, yet the Domesday Book records the existence of a church and priest in the area as far back as 1086. The first accepted reference to the present site can be found in 1333 during the reign of Edward III, when it was declared that the church had been founded by the late thirteenth-century Welshman Trahaearn ap Ithel ap Eunydd and his five brothers.

The structure that existed during this period was built with locally sourced stone, although much of the initial building has been lost to later restructuring. The church that stands today is generally dated to 1492, when it was extensively rebuilt under the instructions of Sir Thomas Stanley, Earl of Derby. Stanley was a powerful noble who controlled the north-west of England with an authority akin to that of a prince. Blessed with an enviable inheritance, Stanley had a strong Yorkist pedigree during the Wars of the Roses, as cousin by marriage to King Edward IV, while his son George had married into the prominent Woodville family of the queen. Despite this, in 1472, he married Lancastrian Margaret Beaufort, the mother of the exiled Henry Tudor, who undoubtedly hoped a marriage to a Yorkist stalwart would help in bringing her boy home.

Although intervention was not initially forthcoming, Stanley famously interceded for his stepson at the Battle of Bosworth in 1485, and decisively turned the battle in the favour of the Tudors. It was even recorded that Stanley himself placed King Richard III's coronet on the head of the new king during the aftermath of the victory. His reward was further endowment from his wife's son, including ennoblement as the Earl of Derby and securing the prestigious office of High Constable of England. Capitalising on her son's authority and utilising her husband's dominance in the north-west, Margaret Beaufort actively helped fund a series of new churches, including Gresford, which received ample financing for renovation.

The size and significance of such a church seems disproportionate to the modern village, but this would have been even more pronounced during the Tudor period, when the presence of this large building among a community of twenty houses would have been dominant to say the least. It is feasible that the magnitude of this church turned it into a place of pilgrimage and may even have inspired some of the donations during the sixteenth century that enabled it to prosper. Robert Parfew, Bishop of St Asaph and a cleric significant enough to be present at the funeral of Queen Jane Seymour in 1537, had even pleaded with Thomas Cromwell to transfer his base to Gresford, in the process enlightening the king's great minister as to the importance of the church and its pilgrimage tradition. Parfew stated, 'Of late time many and divers oblations, offerings, profits and advantages were yearly from divers parts of this Realm brought, given and offered at and in the said church of Gresford.'

Constructed in the perpendicular style that was in vogue during the late fifteenth century, the church features many of the iconic examples of this late Gothic design, from the many large mullioned windows to the large Tudor arched window on the east wall. The imposing tower was built in two stages – the first part, up to the quatrefoil adornment, marks the remains of the fourteenth-century construction, while the latter part was added after 1512, when a local man, John Roden, a Sergeant-at-Arms to the first two Tudor kings, bequeathed money for the extension.

The top of this tower features ogee curves, which contain louvred openings, inside which the bell chamber is situated. The eight bells housed in the chamber are traditionally the reason for the church's inclusion as a 'wonder of Wales'. The pinnacles which adorn the top of the parapet were added in 1582 when another benefactor, John Leach, left ten shillings for their addition. These are accompanied by eight figures, which are supposedly those of kings, knights or pilgrims.

The church features various Tudor motifs that are typical of buildings erected during the period, a by-product of the dynasty's desire to be eternally conspicuous among their subjects. The Tudor rose and the Beaufort portcullis are just two such examples. A stone carving of a crowned male on the buttress of the tower is believed to be that of Henry Tudor, a boastful ornament of this notable scion of the Church's chief benefactors. This is accompanied by a female in what would appear to be the same type of headdress that Margaret Beaufort was noted to wear, although it is not certain that this is meant to depict the king's beloved mother.

All Saints church, Gresford.

John Trevor's tomb, Gresford.

An unusual wall monument can be found in the church commemorating John Trevor of Trevalyn, a local gentleman who died in June 1589. His epitaph in Welsh proudly states that Trevor spent his youthful years fighting for King Henry VIII in his French wars while he then spent his middle age travelling through various countries. His effigy is unusual in that it depicts Trevor lying on his side as opposed to on his back as seems traditional; clearly this was designed to impress his neighbours after death. A further Tudor-related item of interest is the deteriorating sixteenth-century Day of Judgement wall painting that is situated above an arch on the east wall, undoubtedly capturing the attention of the Tudor congregation as they worshipped. The north chapel, meanwhile, possesses stained glass dating from 1498, which portrays the Virgin Mary's life in various stages.

Many churches underwent great change in the centuries that followed the Tudors, to such an extent that it is rare to find authentic sixteenth-century remains that have been unsullied by later architectural restructuring. Fortunately the delightful All Saints church retains an almost unique character that allows one to embrace the experience of a worshipper during the Tudor period, a place for which the term hidden gem could have been conceived.

Gwydir Castle

During the Tudor era, Gwydir Castle enjoyed a reputation among the very finest in Wales with regards to its grandeur as a fortified manor house. Upon visiting, it is understandable why this was the case. The burgeoning Welsh gentry class that had emerged during the early sixteenth century transformed their medieval castles into comfortable residences, and Gwydir underwent this process accordingly, under the ownership of the Wynn family.

Situated across the river from Llanrwst in the scenic Conwy Valley, Gwydir Castle came into the possession of the Wynn family in the late fifteenth century when it was purchased and renovated by Maredudd ap Ieuan ap Robert, a key supporter of King Henry VII and founder of the Wynn dynasty, which would become prominent in the region over the next few centuries.

The castle was further renovated during the 1540s when material was astutely recycled from the nearby Maenan Abbey, which had been dissolved during the Reformation. It was around this period that the square turret to the rear of the Solar Tower was added, while the courtyard gatehouse was built in 1555. The initials of Sir John Wynn can be seen above the solid wooden door. Gwydir was updated once more towards the end of the sixteenth century when an Elizabethan porch was added, complete with a Tudor arch entrance and the ever-present Wynn family coat of arms.

A notable resident of Gwydir was Katherine of Berain, a Welsh heiress lauded by some as a Tudor cousin of Queen Elizabeth I. As her father was Tudor ap Robert Vychan there was some authenticity in her being referred to as Katherine Tudor, but it was through her maternal grandfather, Sir Roland de Velville, that the curious legend of her Tudor heritage persisted. Sir Roland was a Breton who ostensibly arrived in England alongside Henry Tudor in 1485 and remained in the king's favour for the remainder of the reign. The unusualness of this situation – a common Breton soldier treated favourably by the first two Tudor monarchs – raised later rumours that he was in fact an illegitimate son of Henry Tudor from the latter's exile in Brittany; this charge was lent further weight when, in 1512, de Velville was granted the ancestral lands of the Tudors in Penmynydd and the constableship of Beaumaris Castle. His granddaughter Katherine went through four marriages with the elite of North Welsh nobility, including John Salusbury and Sir Richard Clough, although it was her third marriage – to Maurice Wynn, the heir of Sir John – which brought Katherine to Gwydir. She would remain here until her husband's death in 1580. Today the privately owned Gwydir has been faithfully restored and is one of the finest examples of a Tudor mansion in the UK.

Inner courtyard, Gwydir Castle.

Elizabethan porch, Gwydir Castle.

Harlech Castle

'Men of Harlech, march to glory, victory is hov'ring o'er ye' is today one of the most famous opening lines of any song connected with Wales, and it refers to an episode during the Wars of the Roses, whereupon Harlech Castle held out against capture for over seven years in loyalty to Lancastrian commander Jasper Tudor and his half-brother King Henry VI. During the pinnacle of the wars in the early 1460s, the House of Lancaster had been removed from the throne by the Yorkist King Edward IV, and Jasper Tudor had been forced to flee the country. The Earl of Pembroke retained his stature among the Welsh, and ensured that his dependable and faithful adherents stubbornly held Harlech Castle, a defence so successful it would remain the only Lancastrian stronghold throughout England and Wales from 1461 to 1468.

Today considered a World Heritage Site, it is instantly apparent upon arrival at Harlech why this fortress escaped capture for almost a decade. The castle is built upon a large rock almost 200 feet high, which affords the fortress incredible views across the region, with Snowdonia providing a scenic vista. The gatehouse offers an imposing encounter to the visitor, as the entranceway into the inner ward of this concentric stronghold. With four large towers at each corner of the castle, with further reinforcements beyond, it is fathomable why Jasper Tudor and his supporters were able to utilise Harlech in their increasingly desperate cause. The ideal location next to the Irish Sea naturally allowed Jasper easy access to occasionally flee any impending apprehension.

Jasper launched at least one raid into North Wales from this secure location and also inadvertently brought about its surrender when it was rumoured he was about to land at the castle with an invasion force from France. This possibility spurred King Edward IV into action and he authorised a colossal force under Sir William Herbert of Raglan to finally seize the fortress, which was accomplished in 1468. It is a possibility that the eleven-year-old Henry Tudor was present at this capture as part of his military education under Lord Raglan, with whom he had been living as a ward since he was four. Frustratingly for both Herbert and King Edward, Henry's uncle Jasper once more evaded capture and left Harlech by sea, utilising the long, fortified path that led down to the bay. Due to its splendid location and inspiring history, historic Harlech is arguably the most atmospheric site to visit in Wales, a spectacularly stunning spot in the shadows of Snowdonia.

St Winefride's Well, Holywell

St Winefride's Well in Flintshire was once lauded as the 'Lourdes of Wales', and, similar to the French Catholic shrine, welcomed pilgrims from across the country eager to have their ailments cured by divine intervention. It is claimed that St Winefride's Well is the only place of pilgrimage with a continuous history stretching back over thirteen centuries. According to the legend that accompanies the spring, Winefride was a young woman with ambitions to become a nun when local prince Caradog attempted to corrupt her and then take her for his wife.

Having refused the advances of this infatuated prince and valiantly resisted his ardent attempts to rape her, the virtuous Winefride was beheaded by the furious Caradog. It is said that a spring erupted on the spot on which her lifeless head came to rest. Winefride was restored to life after the prayers of her uncle St Bueno, and she spent the remainder of her days serving God as the nun she had always wished to be. Since these alleged events took place in the seventh century, St Winefride has been venerated among Catholics, with her eponymous well receiving royal patronage throughout the centuries, including from the Tudors. A statue depicting her can be found in the Henry VII Lady chapel at Westminster Abbey.

As principal landowner in north-east Wales and nearby Cheshire through her husband Thomas Stanley, it is unsurprising to learn that the pious Lady Margaret Beaufort took great interest in the spring at Holywell and ordered the construction of a chapel above the well that is very much in the image of other Beaufort churches in the locality, like Gresford or Mold. The Gothic perpendicular building was erected around the start of the sixteenth century to replace an earlier building, and was designed to not only serve as a comfortable place of worship for pilgrims but to demonstrate the ascendancy of the Tudor dynasty.

The source of the water is situated in an open crypt below the chapel, the water bubbling into a pool shaped like an eight-pointed star, then flowing into an external bathing pool added at a later date. The pilgrim would enter into the watery basin via the steps, before exiting the spring and circling the well three times. Margaret ensured that all visitors in the late fifteenth and early sixteenth century understood that the well enjoyed the patronage of the Tudor dynasty, of which her son was the first monarch. The most prominent display of this benefaction is the protruding boss that emerges from the fan-vaulted roof directly above the well, which not only has a sculptured depiction of Winefride's life but also displays the Tudor royal coat of arms on the base. The remainder of the crypt is richly adorned with the heraldic symbols of both Henry VII and his stepfather Thomas Stanley, in addition to those of Katherine of Aragon. High on the ceiling to the right of the well is a weathered stone depiction of Lady Margaret and Lord Stanley, while the Tudor dragon and Richmond greyhound can be observed above the crypt entrance archway.

In spite of her support, St Winefride's suffered at the hands of Lady Margaret's grandson King Henry VIII in 1540, when he ordered the shrine to be destroyed during the process of the tumultuous Reformation, with many saintly relics casually destroyed in the process. The structure itself remained undamaged, however, and today is a Grade I listed building open to pilgrims of all faiths.

Pendant boss and fan-vaulted roof, St Winefride's Well.

St Winefride's church.

St Mary's Church, Mold

St Mary's church in the centre of Mold is a further example of a Stanley church in north-east Wales, financed by Thomas Stanley and his wife Margaret Beaufort, matriarch of the Tudor dynasty. Constructed in a similar perpendicular style to that of its sister church at Gresford, it has been thought that this building campaign in the region was a thanksgiving operation in the aftermath of the Tudor victory at Bosworth. Although an earlier church existed at the site, it was reconstructed by Stanley and Beaufort early in the Tudor reign, and their influence can still be seen today in the stained glass. The window which adjoins the entrance displays the Stanley badge, while the glass above the vestry door proudly incorporates the Legs of Mann, the triskelion symbol that the Stanley earls used to highlight their titular claim to the Isle of Man.

The panels above the vestry also commemorate two Tudor-period characters, with the left honouring Vicar Ellis ap David while the right panel paid tribute to Edward Stanley, 3rd Earl of Derby and great-grandson of the 1st earl. Edward was an integral member of King Henry VIII's court as a young man, and not only assisted the powerful Cardinal Wolsey in affairs of state but travelled to Rome in 1530 to present the disapproving Pope Clement VII with documents highlighting the king's desire to divorce his wife Katherine of Aragon. He remained a member of the Royal Household under King Henry's three children, Edward VI, Mary I and Elizabeth I, before dying in 1572. While not possessing the tomb of Ruabon or the majesty of Gresford, St Mary's in Mold is still worth a visit when in the locality for its Stanley, and by extension Tudor, links.

Mold church.

Penmynydd

While Pembroke Castle has a valid claim as the birthplace of the Tudor dynasty, to many North Walians the true origin of England's most famous ruling family is a quiet, unassuming village on the rural island of Anglesey. Penmynydd, literally 'top of the mountain', lies on the B5420 road between the Menai Bridge and the town of Llangefni. With a lack of signs indicating where you are, it is possible to drive through the few houses that constitute Penmynydd without realising the historical importance of the hamlet through which you have just traversed.

Although it may not be discernable to the casual visitor, Penmynydd was the base from which one of Wales's most powerful families grew into Britain and Europe's most notorious dynasty. The family that would become known as the Tudors began its mercurial rise with the accomplishments of Ednyfed Fychan, the thirteenth-century seneschal to the great Gwynedd princes. As steward and chancellor to Llywelyn the Great, Ednyfed was a valued and loyal servant to his prince and, as expected, was well rewarded in riches and land. Among his acquisitions was the Lordship of Penmynydd, which would become both his and his descendants' power base; from here, they imposed their influence on the politics of the region. After the kingdom was conquered in 1282 by King Edward I of England, Ednyfed's heirs ensured they maintained their grip on power by developing an understanding with the English officials and remaining firmly among the native elite in Gwynedd.

Ednyfed's descendants reached their zenith of power in North Wales under his great-great-great-grandchildren, the anachronistically termed Tudors of Penmynydd. This tight-knit clan of five brothers were born to Tudur ap Goronwy, and all would flourish towards the end of the fourteenth century as loyal servants to King Richard II. The eldest son was probably Goronwy Fychan ap Tudur, who became Forrester of Snowdonia in 1382 as well as attaining the remarkable position of Constable of Beaumaris Castle shortly before his death from drowning. The lands he owned at Penmynydd passed to his brothers, each of whom had his own lands and positions of authority elsewhere on the island of Anglesey.

After Richard II was usurped by Henry Bolingbroke, the remaining sons of Tudur swiftly became rebels when they joined their cousin Owain Glyndŵr in campaigning against the new king, in what would become known as the War of Independence. Although another son – Ednyfed – had followed Goronwy to the grave by this point, Gwilym, Rhys and Maredudd ap Tudur allied themselves with their ferocious cousin in a strategy that would bring short-term success before leaving the family inheritance utterly destroyed. The brothers captured Conwy Castle in a daring raid in 1401 and were probably present at Glyndŵr's first parliament in 1404. After French assistance failed to materialise, the sheer might of the English army eventually crushed the Welsh rebellion, and Rhys in particular would suffer the pain of a traitor's death when he was publicly executed by being hanged, drawn and quartered in Shrewsbury.

Maredudd ap Tudur was the youngest of the band of brothers and would end his days as an outlaw after escaping into the unforgiving wilderness that was Snowdonia, although not before fathering a young son, Owain. Due to the actions of these Tudurs during the rebellion, their influence in North Welsh politics from their base in Penmynydd came to a grinding halt, the lands passing to a distant cousin as a reward for his early submission to the English. With his disgraced father and uncles dead and the family inheritance lost, young Owain ap Maredudd ap Tudur was forced to leave his ancestral home in order to seek a living, and ostensibly arrived in London to this purpose. It was through his incredibly unlikely union with Katherine of Valois, dowager queen of King Henry V, that Edmund and Jasper Tudor were born. The two siblings were brought up as members of the Lancastrian royal family, to which they were now related as half-brothers of King Henry VI. It would be Edmund's son Henry, a grandson of the Penmynydd Tudors, who would ascend to the throne of England in 1485 as King Henry VII. In three generations this minor Penmynydd family had emerged from near ruin to become the most powerful family on the British Isles, with a fame that still resonates worldwide 500 years later.

There are two sites of interest in the village of Penmynydd, namely Plas Penmynydd and St Gredifael's church. The current house that stands at Plas Penmynydd is a later construction than the one that would have been known by the thirteenth- and fourteenth-century Tudors, built during the reign of their progeny Elizabeth I in 1576 and further renovated during the following century. The estate is now a private Grade II listed home, but is not currently accessible to the public. A fleur-de-lis engraving, an emblem of the French-born Katherine of Valois, has been unearthed inside, while the present owner has ensured the Tudor coat of arms is prominent on the façade of the current building.

St Gredifael's is an active parish church and therefore remains open to the public as the village's place of worship. It is said to have been founded as a Celtic church by the Breton Saint Gredifael in the sixth century, with the first stone church being constructed in the twelfth century when the area was still under the rule of the princes of Gwynedd. The current incarnation of St Gredifael's dates from around the fourteenth century when it would have been the local religious house for the various inhabitants of Plas Penmynydd, and can be found about half a mile north of the village between the junctions of two minor backstreet roads. It was here, in the shadow of Snowdonia, that Goronwy ap Tudur was buried in the 1380s after his untimely death from drowning, and his impressive alabaster tomb can still be admired.

As Owen Tudor's paternal uncle, Goronwy would become a great-great uncle to the King of England and related to every British monarch since. The late fourteenth-century tomb displays an effigy of Goronwy next to his wife Myfanwy in the north chapel of the church, since renamed the Tudor Chapel. Five shields can be viewed on each side, with two on the ends, although the coats of arms have long since weathered with time. Clothed in a medieval surcoat with his head covered in chainmail and legs resting upon a lion, the handless Goronwy appears every inch the soldier and knight that he aspired to be.

A stained-glass window in the chapel contains prominent Tudor symbolism, including the Tudor rose and Beaufort portcullis. The border of the window reads, '*Undeb fel rhosyn yw ar lan afonydd ac fel ty dur ar ben y mynydd,*' which translates as 'unity is like a rose on a river bank, and like a House of Steel on the top of a mountain'. The two metaphors that may not seem immediately obvious to the reader are 'top of a mountain'/'*ben y mynydd*', which refers to Penmynydd itself and the more obscure 'house of steel'/'*ty dur*' reference, which represents the Tudors. Elsewhere in the church, the edge of the pews bear the French royal symbol of the fleur-de-lis, which represents the union of the Tudors to the French royal family through Owen Tudor's morganatic marriage with Katherine of Valois.

Penmynydd is a tiny hamlet that does not broadcast its Tudor connection yet does not shy away from this remarkably unique link to the island's most famous family. Although Plas Penmynydd is a private estate and naturally does not invite the attention of tourists, St Gredifael's church remains open year round and welcomes visitors to view the Tudor chapel. Any visit to the north-east of Wales warrants a trip across the Menai Strait to explore the village where, it could be argued, the seeds of the British Empire were first sown.

St Gredifael's church, Penmynydd.

St Mary's Church, Ruabon

St Mary's church is a perpendicular-styled construction in the community of Ruabon, and is home to a splendid Tudor tomb of an obscure Welsh knight. The Grade I listed church has undergone consistent renovation over the centuries, but still maintains some of its sixteenth-century charm. The church has architectural features from before the Tudor ascendancy, including the fourteenth-century tower, but it is the interior of the building that singles out St Mary's as relevant to the Tudor enthusiast.

In the North Chapel is sited one of the finest surviving examples of a Tudor-era tomb in Wales: the monumental effigy of loyal Tudor servant, John ap Elis Eyton. This local member of the gentry first came to wider prominence at the landmark Battle of Bosworth in 1485 when, similar to many Welshmen, he declared for the rebel Henry Tudor against the forces of King Richard III. It was a wise decision, and upon the accession of his compatriot to the throne he found himself rewarded with various estates in the Ruabon area. In addition John was further rewarded with an annuity of ten marks from a grateful King Henry VII, 'in consideration of the time and faithful service performed for us in the course of our triumphal victory'. Although this knight may be relatively unknown outside of his native locale, his indicative importance to the Ruabon area can be acknowledged from the relative extravagance of his tomb. Although weathered by time, coat of arms shields along the base offer a visual record of the family connections to John ap Elis Eyton, while he himself is adorned with the SS Collar, a symbol of the House of Lancaster and suggestive of his adherence to Henry Tudor. The Latin inscription on the tomb pleads with the visitor to 'pray for the souls of John ap Elis Eyton, knight who died on September 28, 1526 and Elizabeth Calveley his wife, who died in 1524'.

A further Tudor connection that this unassuming church possesses is that David Powel, the noted antiquarian who published the first printed history of Wales, 'A Historie of Cambria', in 1584, was the Vicar of Ruabon from 1570 to 1578. Powel was a typical Elizabethan Renaissance man who diligently assisted other writers of the period in their own literary pursuits, including Bishop William Morgan in his translation of the Bible into Welsh. His own piece of work was noted for embellishment in parts, notably his account of Prince Madoc of Gwynedd's alleged discovery of America in the twelfth century. This traditional tale of the son of a Welsh king discovering America over three centuries before Columbus was utilised as Elizabethan propaganda in the escalating colonial conflict with the Spanish, with writers like Powel keen to emphasise Elizabeth's descent from the ancient Welsh kings and thus her right to claim America on their behalf. Powel also enjoyed lengthy friendships with Dr John Dee and Blanche Parry, favourites at the court of Queen Elizabeth I, and ensured he enjoyed a degree of royal patronage. The church which Powel once served may have no permanent memorial to a Tudor-era Welshman of substantial significance, but nonetheless Ruabon allows the visitor to experience the existence of the Tudors in a rural, regional sense, away from the larger and more important settlements.

Tomb of John ap Elis Eyton, Ruabon.

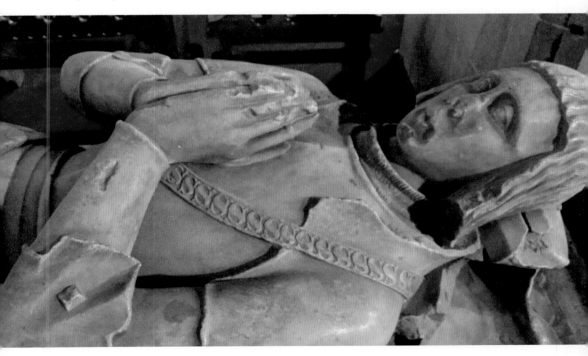

John ap Elis Eyton.

Tŷ Mawr Wybrnant

Tŷ Mawr is a spectacularly situated farmhouse in the picturesque Wybrnant valley, notable as the birthplace of William Morgan, celebrated translator of the Welsh Bible and one of the most influential Welshmen in history. Morgan had utilised the patronage of the Wynns of Gwydir to attain a top-level education at St John's College, Cambridge, and returned home to embark on a successful clerical career. His translation was completed by 1587, and went on to become remarkably popular among his fellow countrymen, a masterpiece which has endured to the present day.

Roughly 3 miles south-west of Betws-y-Coed and approached via a scenic forest road, the present Tŷ Mawr building was rebuilt in the late Elizabethan period to expand on the simple hall in which Bishop Morgan had been born in 1545, including the addition of a more efficient fireplace and larger upper chambers for the inhabitants. Maintained by the National Trust, the flowers outside the farmhouse are sixteenth century, an authentic if detailed addition to the idyllic surroundings, enhanced by the small stone bridge which provides access across the small Wybrnant stream. Inside, a collection of antique furniture helpfully assists in setting the scene, while worthy of investigation are the collection of Bibles on show, in particular Morgan's own 1588 edition, one of only twenty known copies in existence. A slate plaque, fittingly in Welsh, commemorates William Morgan's birth and translation.

Tŷ Mawr Wybrnant.

St Giles's Church, Wrexham

Situated in the heart of the largest town in North Wales, the splendid St Giles's church with its soaring tower is presently renowned as the location of Elihu Yale's tomb; the American-born merchant was credited with aiding in the foundation of the eponymous university in Connecticut, USA. The church is widely held to be among the greatest of the medieval buildings still standing in Wales and is considered to be one of the 'Seven Wonders of Wales', a distinction it shares with the church at nearby Gresford.

St Giles's possesses a great tower constructed in the perpendicular style of the early sixteenth century, and was assembled in place of the previous tower, which burned down in 1463. Redeveloped under the orders of the Earl of Derby and his wife Margaret Beaufort, St Giles's is considered to be another Stanley redevelopment in this north-east corner of Wales, due to its similarity in style and architecture to others like Gresford and Mold. The erection of the eye-catching tower commenced in 1506 and was completed by 1524, remaining elevated high above Wrexham for five centuries.

Standing an impressive 135 feet tall, the tower is adorned with many examples of medieval carving, among later Victorian ornamentations. One of the statues on the north wall portrays St James the Great, patron saint of travellers and of Spain, and it is thought to have been commissioned in celebration of King Henry VIII's marriage to Katherine of Aragon in 1509. The west wall contains a thick wooden door with prominent Tudor emblems carved onto the gate, notably the Beaufort portcullis flanked by the Tudor rose. The chancel and high altar were also added to the existing structure, which increased the overall length of the church to 178 feet. It was clearly designed to be another expensive and conspicuous display of Tudor propaganda in an area already replete with familial connections.

Inside the church there are three Tudor connections in particular to be noted. The first, and certainly the most noticeable, is the sixteenth-century camber beam timber roof in the nave, an example of Tudor craftsmanship that has remained as durable as the day it was erected. There is also a collection of corbels of varying designs situated underneath the roof, which add to its aesthetic, predictably including Tudor roses and the Beaufort portcullis. Noticeable directly underneath the roof and over the east wall arch is an early Tudor wall painting which depicts the Day of Judgement. The artwork was only rediscovered in the nineteenth century.

St Giles's also possesses a rare brass lectern that is considered to date from 1524 and thus is pre-Reformation in origin. The lectern, the stand from which the speaker would deliver their sermon, is in the design of an eagle, a common motif found in churches prior to the reforming of the English Church under Henry VIII and his son Edward VI. The eagle was considered to encompass symbolism favourable to the medieval worshipper, its propensity for flying at high altitudes, for example, denoting its closeness to the Kingdom of Heaven. The brass wings of the St Giles's eagle would provide support for the placing of the Bible in preparation for the reciter addressing the congregation, and is certainly lavish in design. It is said to have been presented to the church by a lady named Matilda, the daughter of John ap Gruffydd of Plas-y-Stiwart, who bequeathed the lectern to St Giles's in his will. The badly damaged effigy of Hugh Bellot is also located in the chancel, a worn memorial to this Elizabethan scholar who served as Bishop of Bangor and Chester from 1585 to 1596.

Close to where the lectern is traditionally placed is the third item of note: a bust of Margaret Beaufort, complete with crown atop her head, emphasising her exalted position as the king's mother. The presence of the bust only serves to reinforce the Stanley–Beaufort connection with St Giles's and helps establish the undoubted importance the newly ascended royal dynasty placed on this regional parish church. There is another intriguing bust across the nave, which possibly depicts her husband Thomas Stanley, although this portrayal curiously appears to be adorned with donkey ears. St Giles's parish church still commandingly rises above the largest town in North Wales 500 years after its rebuilding, and it is a delightful example of Tudor architecture playing an integral role in establishing the dynasty outside London.

St Giles's tower, Wrexham.

Pre-Reformation eagle lectern.

Margaret Beaufort corbel, Wrexham.

St John's Church, Ysbyty Ifan

Ysbyty Ifan, or John's Hospital, is a small village in the Wybrnant valley which is home to St John's, the local parish church, with unexpected connections to the Battle of Bosworth and Cardinal Wolsey. There has been a place of worship on this spot since the late twelfth century when a hospice was established by the Knights of St John of Jerusalem, although disappointingly the current building is a Victorian construction.

The church houses memorials to two prominent Tudor characters of this region: Rhys ap Maredudd Fawr and his son Robert ap Rhys. The senior figure gained prestige during the Bosworth campaign when he actively recruited soldiers for the cause of Henry Tudor in North Wales, pledging vital Welsh support to bolster Tudor's primarily Franco-Scottish invading force. Rhys also participated in the battle and was noted for raising the Red Dragon standard on the battlefield after the Tudor standard-bearer Sir William Brandon had been killed. Welsh chroniclers stated that Rhys himself was responsible for the notorious death of King Richard III, cutting down the desperate monarch with a halberd in the vicious fighting that precipitated a change of royal dynasty.

Rhys ap Maredudd's timely support for his fellow Welshman earned him ample rewards from an appreciative King Henry VII, and as a result the family secured their position among the elite of the Welsh gentry classes. Rhys's son Robert was able to capitalise on this goodwill and migrated to London to become a personal chaplain to the mighty Cardinal Thomas Wolsey, a consummate intriguer who famously became England's *alter rex* during the early years of King Henry VIII's colourful reign. It is also probable that Robert came into contact with another of Wolsey's underlings in Thomas Cromwell, who would replace the disgraced cardinal as the premier councillor of the realm.

Effigies to both these men can still be observed within St John's, permanent if weathered memorials to two prosperous North Welsh Tudor personalities. Naturally Rhys is adorned in armour, with a sword resting by his side, while his son wears the religious robes typical of his career as a priest. It seems somewhat tragic that the effigy of Rhys, the soldier who valiantly fought at Bosworth, has suffered such significant damage that only the torso remains. An unidentified yet richly dressed woman joins father and son; she has often been identified as Rhys's wife Lowri, although it may in fact be Robert's spouse Mared.

Bibliography

Alister Williams, W., *The Parish Church of St Giles, Wrexham*, Wrexham: Bridge Books 2000

Avent, R., *Laugharne Castle*, Cardiff: Cadw 1995

Breverton, T., *Owain Glyndwr, The Story of the Last Prince of Wales*, Stroud: Amberley Publishing 2009

Davies, J., *A History of Wales*, London: Penguin Books 2007

Davies, M., *The Story of Tenby*, Tenby: Tenby Museum 1979

Evans, H. T., *Wales and the Wars of the Roses*, Cambridge: Cambridge University Press 1915

Evans, R. E. H., *The Parish Church, Llanwenog*, Port Talbot: D. W. Jones Printers 2007

Griffiths, R. A. & Thomas, R. S., *The Making of the Tudor Dynasty*, Stroud: Sutton Publishing 2005

Gwyn Thomas, W., *St Mary's Parish Church, A Short Account of the Building and History*, Tenby: The Printman 2009

Jenkins, S., *Wales Churches, Houses, Castles*, London: Penguin Books 2011

Kenyon, J. R., *Raglan Castle*, Cardiff: Cadw 2003

Ludlow, N., *Carmarthen Castle*, Carmarthen: Carmarthenshire County Council 2007

Ludlow, N., *Pembroke Castle, Birthplace of the Tudor Dynasty*, Pembroke Dock: Pembroke Castle Trust 2001

Merrony, M. W., *An Official History of Tenby*, Tenby 2004

Norton, E., *Margaret Beaufort, Mother of the Tudor Dynasty*, Stroud: Amberley Publishing 2010

Rees, D., *The Son of Prophecy, Henry Tudor's Road to Bosworth*, Ruthin: John Jones Publishing 1997

Skidmore, C., *Bosworth, The Birth of the Tudors*, London: Weidenfeld & Nicolson 2013

St Fagans: National History Museum Visitor Guide, Cardiff: Amgueddfa Cymru – National Museum Wales 1998

Taylor, A., *Harlech Castle*, Cardiff: Cadw 2007

The Royal Commission on the Ancient and Historical Monuments and Constructions in Wales and Monmouthshire, *An Inventory of the Ancient Monuments in Wales and Monmouthshire: V – County of Carmarthen*, London: His Majesty's Stationary Office 1917

Thomas, H., *A History of Wales 1485–1660*, University of Wales Press 1972

Turner, R., *Lamphey Bishop's Palace Llawhaden Castle*, Cardiff: Cadw 2000

Turner, R., *Plas Mawr, Conwy*, Cardiff: Cadw 2008

Turvey, R., *The Wars of the Roses and Henry VII: Britain 1450–1509*, Hodder Education 2010

Walker, R. G., *Jasper Tudor and the Town of Tenby*, National Library of Wales Journal XVI 1959

Williams, G., *Henry Tudor and Wales*, Cardiff: University of Wales Press 1985

Acknowledgements

I have been told that the acknowledgements page is often the most difficult part of the book for many authors; such is the difficulty in recognising all who have assisted in the journey to publication. Therefore I would like to offer apologies to anyone I may have missed. I would like to offer my full gratitude to those individuals who have played a part in putting the book together, through their direct or indirect involvement with the project. In particular I would like to thank Nicola Gale, Emily Brewer and the rest of the team at Amberley for transforming my amateur hobby into a professional work. I am deeply indebted to you all. Furthermore I would like to thank those who provided me on-location assistance and aid with photograph permissions. Thanks to Ruth Nicholls of Cardiff Castle; Rector Jonathan Smith of St Marcella's church, Denbigh; Jon Williams of Pembroke Castle; Reverend Leigh Richardson of St Mary's church, Carmarthen; Judy and Peter Welford of Gwydir Castle; Carew Castle; Reverend Andrew Davies of St Mary's church, Tenby; the Dean & Chapter of Llandaff Cathedral; the Dean & Chapter of St David's Cathedral; Gerwyn Edwards of Ty Mawr Wybrnant; Berwyn Thomas of Ruabon church; and Dr Cyril Jones. I would also like to extend my gratitude to St Fagans National History Museum, the National Trust and Cadw for the crucial work they do in maintaining and restoring our heritage. Suffice to say all errors are the sole responsibility of the author.

This book would not have been possible without the support, guidance and general good humour of my family and friends. I would like to personally thank my mother Michelle, father Mohammed, and sisters Nadia and Yasmin for providing a home of happy memories. It's been quite a journey and you have provided me with a stable base from which to flourish. Finally I would like to thank Katherine, the person who has become my sole inspiration in life. Your encouragement and support has ensured the realisation of a dream. With you, all is possible.

Selected Contact Details

Carew Castle
Carew
Pembrokeshire
SA70 8SL
Tel: 01646 651782

Lamphey Bishop's Palace
Lamphey
Pembrokeshire
SA71 5JL
Tel: 01646 672224

Pembroke Castle
Pembroke
Pembrokeshire
SA71 4LA
Tel: 01646 684585
Web: www.pembroke-castle.co.uk

St David's Cathedral
The Close
St David's
Pembrokeshire
SA62 6RD
Tel: 01437 720202
Web: www.stdavidscathedral.org.uk

Tenby Tudor Merchant's House
Quay Hill
Tenby
Pembrokeshire
SA70 7BX
Tel: 01834 842279
Web: www.nationaltrust.org.uk/tudor-
merchants-house

Cardiff Castle
Castle Street
Cardiff
CF10 3RB
Tel: 02920 878100
Web: www.cardiffcastle.com

Raglan Castle
Raglan
Usk
NP15 2BT
Tel: 01291 690228

St Fagans
Cardiff
CF5 6XB
Tel: 02920 573500
Web: www.museumwales.ac.uk

Plas Mawr
High Street
Conwy
LL32 8DE
Tel: 01492 580167

Gwydir Castle
Llanrwst
Conwy
LL26 0PN
Tel: 01492 641687
Web: www.gwydircastle.co.uk

St Winefride's Well
Holywell
Flintshire
CH8 7PN
Tel: 01352 713054
Web: www.saintwinefrideswell.com

Tŷ Mawr Wybrnant
Penmachno
Betws-y-Coed
LL25 0HJ
Tel: 01690 760213
Web: www.nationaltrust.org.uk/ty-mawr-
wybrnant

Raglan
Castle.

More Kings & Queens from Amberley Publishing

THE TUDORS
Richard Rex

'The best introduction to England's most important dynasty'
DAVID STARKEY

£9.99   978-1-4456-0700-9   272 pages PB 143 illus, 66 col

KATHARINE OF ARAGON
Patrick Williams

'Williams has the courage to march in where most biographers have feared to tread'
SARAH GRISTWOOD, BBC HISTORY MAGAZINE

£25.00   978-1-84868-325-9   512 pages HB 70 col illus

RICHARD III
David Baldwin

'A believably complex Richard, neither wholly villain nor hero'
PHILIPPA GREGORY

£9.99   978-1-4456-1591-2   296 pages PB 80 illus, 60 col

WILLIAM THE CONQUEROR
Peter Rex

'Rex has a real ability to communicate difficult issues to a wide audience'
BBC HISTORY MAGAZINE

£12.99   978-1-4456-0698-9   304 pages PB 43 illus, 30 col

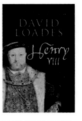

ENGLAND'S QUEENS: THE BIOGRAPHY
Elizabeth Norton

'A truly enlightening read' **THEANNEBOLEYNFILES.COM**

£16.99   978-1-4456-0904-1   432 pages PB 241 illus, 184 col

CATHERINE PARR
Elizabeth Norton

'Norton cuts an admirably clear path through tangled Tudor intrigues'
JENNY UGLOW, THE FINANCIAL TIMES

£9.99   978-1-4456-0383-4   304 pages PB 49 illus, 39 col

HENRY VIII
David Loades

'David Loades Tudor biographies are both highly enjoyable and instructive, the perfect combination' **ANTONIA FRASER**

£12.99   978-1-4456-0704-7   512 pages PB 113 illus, 49 col

ANNE BOLEYN
Lacey Baldwin Smith

'The perfect introduction'
SUZANNAH LIPSCOMB, BBC HISTORY MAGAZINE

£20.00   978-1-4456-1023-8   240 pages HB 60 illus, 40 col

THE KINGS AND QUEENS OF ENGLAND
David Loades

£25.00   978-1-4456-0582-1
512 pages HB   200 illus, 150 col

ELFRIDA
Elizabeth Norton

£20.00   978-1-4456-1486-1
224 pages HB   40 illus

ELIZABETH OF YORK
Amy Licence

£20.00   978-1-4456-0961-4
272 pages HB   40 illus, 10 col

EDWARD THE CONFESSOR
Peter Rex

£12.99   978-1-4456-0476-3
256 pages PB   30 col illus

Also available as ebooks
Available from all good bookshops or to order direct
Please call **01453-847-800 www.amberleybooks.com**